ASIA LOOKS AT WESTERN CHRISTIANITY

ASIA LOOKS AT
WESTERN CHRISTIANITY

BY THOMAS OHM

HERDER AND HERDER

THIS ENGLISH TRANSLATION BY IRENE MARINOFF
IS BASED ON THE ORIGINAL VERSION OF
"ASIENS KRITIK AM ABENDLÄNDISCHEN CHRISTENTUM"
PUBLISHED BY KÖSEL VERLAG, MÜNCHEN, 1948

SECOND IMPRESSION PUBLISHED 1959 BY
HERDER AND HERDER, INC.,
7 WEST 46th STREET, NEW YORK 36, N.Y.

IMPRIMI POTEST:
✝ HEINRICH SUSO BRECHTER, O.S.B., ERZABT.
ST. OTTILIEN, DEN 5. JUNI 1959

NIHIL OBSTAT: ADRIANUS VAN VLIET, S.T.D.
CENSOR DEPUTATUS.

IMPRIMATUR: E. MORROGH BERNARD. VIC. GEN.
WESTMONASTERII, DIE 29a MAII, 1959

LIBRARY OF CONGRESS CATALOG CARD NUMBER: 59-11368
© 1959 BY HERDER KG
MADE AND PRINTED BY HERDER DRUCK
FREIBURG, WEST GERMANY

LIST OF CONTENTS

LIST OF CONTENTS

LIST OF ABBREVIATIONS

CJC	*Codex Juris Canonici.*
Denz	H. Denzinger, *Enchiridion Symbolorum.*
	Editio 21.–23. Friburgi Brisg., 1937.
EMZ	*Evangelische Missions-Zeitschrift.*
EIsl	*Shorter Encyclopaedia of Islam,* edited by H. A. R.
	Gibb and J. H. Kramers. Leiden and London, 1953.
EncIsl	*The Encyclopaedia of Islam.* Leiden and London,
	1913–38.
ERE	Hasting's *Encyclopaedia of Religion and Ethics.*
IRM	*International Review of Missions.*
Mon. Germ.	*Monumenta Germaniae.*
NZM	*Neue Zeitschrift für Missionswissenschaft.*
ZMR	*Zeitschrift für Missionswissenschaft und Religions-*
	wissenschaft.

PREFACE

THE request for a preface to this book comes a few days before my departure for lectures in the United States. So my inclination was to plead shortness of time. In fact, I am glad to have had the chance to read the book and to commend it cordially.

The "salesman" of Christian pearls to-day in the East has, if he is European, difficulty in even getting to the lands of his customers, or being allowed to stay there. To work there with profit is often harder still. Why this is so and what Christians can do to make Christianity acceptable is the theme of Father Ohm's book. Its usefulness goes far beyond his contribution to Mission knowledge and policy. The obstacles met by the modern missionary are due, in great part, to mistakes in the past now recogniced but very hard to repair. For instance, our modern insistence on the separation between Christians and European "colonial" interests is a condition of survival to-day; that these interests coincided far too closely not long ago is not readily forgotten in the East. Not forgotten either is the attitude, once too common, of indiscriminating contempt for non-Christian religions. As missionaries who sought out and built upon the elements of truth were often suspect to their brethren, so now the more general recognition of such elements seems to the Easterner now in power a convenient afterthought, a policy of expediency.

If our Lord is to be truly known and loved in our own West, we must note that much the same type of mistake as in the East has been made repeatedly, for instance, where the Church has lost the working classes.

With us, self-criticism is not yet a condition of survival. It may become so if we remain for too long complacent and self-satisfied.

London,
May 1958

† T. D. Roberts, S. J.
Archbishop of Sygdia, late of Bombay

INTRODUCTION

AT the present time we Christians of the West are passing through manifold and terrible dangers and tribulations, distress and anxiety, upheavals and crises, interior even more than exterior. Not only have ancient churches and chapels collapsed or are threatened with collapse, but also old-established orders and traditions. Not only material strongholds have been lost or are being lost, but also strongholds of the mind and of the spirit. In many parts of Asia Christians are in danger and their missions have been destroyed. In others the situation is critical. Practically nowhere are the times favourable. Attacks on Christianity and its missions are more numerous and violent than ever. Small wonder then that many Christians are disappointed and have lost their self-confidence; small wonder, too, that many remember the past only with anxiety, and envisage the future with uncertainty. Why did it all happen? Was it bound to come? Would it also have happened if we had understood and lived Christianity according to the intentions of Christ? There are not a few who would answer these questions in the negative and act accordingly. Some turn their backs on Western forms of Christianity or even on Christianity itself. Others, however, seek a better, a genuine understanding of Christ's message and of his work, and call for a refashioning or transformation of our Christian life, a resurrection, a rebirth of Christ in us and among us.

Among the latter there are some who expect a proper understanding of Christianity, and with it the basis for its renewal, to come from men distant from ourselves, from the inhabitants of the Continent whence Christianity arose. This leads to an inquiry into Eastern opinions and views of Western Christianity in general, and of the interpretation and realization of the message and ideals of Jesus by Europeans in particular. To-day, as men did two thousand years ago in Rome during its decline, the perplexed and bewildered West is looking towards the East. *Ex Oriente lux!*

Inquiries into the meaning and justification, the content and value of Christianity, however, do not provide all that is necessary for the explanation and justification of our subject. World history, it is true, is not, as Bachofen maintained, "essentially a struggle between East and West". All the same that struggle constitutes an essential element in world history. At the very least it plays an important part in the mighty upheavals that are going on at the present time. Meanwhile relations between the largest continent and Europe have entered a new phase. To-day Asia has come closer to us than would have been thought possible even a short time ago. In his judgement on Europe, God is also using the East as an instrument.

At the moment the effect of this development on our religion cannot be assessed. Its importance for Christianity, however, can hardly be overestimated. In 1939, a European could write: "No longer and not yet again are vital decisions made in Asia; our Continent is still the heart of the world."[1] But to-day those appear to have been right who were convinced that the destiny of mankind, and especially religious and spiritual questions, the fate of Christianity among them, would be decided in the East. "It is in Asia – not in America, or Europe or Africa – that the future of the Christian religion will be determined, is determined."[2]

In the following chapters I shall attempt to give an answer to these questions. I regard as "Asians" in the first instance the inhabitants of India, of Siam, Burma, Malaya, of Central Asia, the Far East and the south-east Asian archipelago: Hindus, Buddhists, Confucians, Taoists, Shintoists – that is those Asians who up to modern times have developed their cast of mind and their spiritual life

[1] W. Kiechler, *Dionysos, Prometheus, Christos* (Krailling, 1939), p. 70.
[2] O. Buck, *Christianity Tested* (New York, 1934).

on more or less purely Asian lines or in complete independence from Europe. I am including Moslem Orientals and the inhabitants of Northern Asia to a lesser degree, since they are more closely related to us in spirit and have for many centuries been subjected to European influences. Yet they, as well as Asian Christians, will be heard.

In this context "the West" and "Europe" signify the Catholic, Protestant and secularized parts of Western Europe and America; "Western" or "European" Christianity: the Christian faith as it is preached, represented, lived and realized by the Christians and "Christian nations" of the West, with all its essential features, universal as well as European, human as well as divine.

In this context many will miss a clear distinction between Christianity and Western Christianity. They might argue that the title of the book is misleading. It only mentions Western Christianity. In actual fact, however, Christianity of the West in all its component parts is the issue. But, many things which we firmly believe to be originally, essentially and universally Christian – for example, our doctrine of the transcendence of God – are regarded in Asia as intrinsically European. There are even many who consider the whole of contemporary Christianity as something more or less purely European. Consequently I include the whole of Western Christianity, even those elements which are not genuinely in the range of my study.

But is it possible to regard "Western Christianity" as a closed entity and to pass collective verdicts? Is not Western Christianity a colourful mosaic of thoughts and doctrines, ideals and forms of life, of attitudes and orders? Does not Lutheranism differ from Calvinism and Catholicism, not to mention the various trends in individual denominations? These are quite sensible questions. But as Christians pass collective verdicts on Paganism, Buddhism, Islam, so do Asians on European Christianity. Consequently we may inquire into these collective verdicts. Whether they are correct is, of course, a different matter. Moreover, in spite of all its differences and tensions, Western Christianity is, precisely like the West itself, to a certain degree a unity and an entity. The differences and tensions are an essential part of Western Christianity.

I am fully conscious of the difficulties of the task. To-day it is less difficult than before to find out what Asians think, really think, what their true aim is, what their innermost feelings are. To-day many Asians tell us openly, even brutally, what they think of Christianity. Yet Asians of the old school remain very courteous and do not always express their opinions lest they should displease us. After a performance of Wagner's *Rienzi* in New York, an

Indian shook his head and said politely to his European friend: "It must have been very beautiful." If, to quote an example, the old Chinese world strikes the modern Chinese of materialistic mentality as very mysterious, how unfathomable must it be for us Occidentals! We shall never reach a complete understanding of a genuine Asian.

A further difficulty lies in the multiplicity and variety of conceptions. The Indian way of thought is different from the Arab, the Mongol different from the Malayan. Japanese spirituality stands out in sharp contrast to Korean. Islam and Buddhism do not share the same opinions and scales of values. Even within individual peoples and religions we find widely divergent views. I was told in the East that it is, for instance, quite absurd to talk of the mentality of the Japanese. The Hinayana-Buddhist and the Amidist follow very different standards, and the same applies to orthodox and modernist Moslems. To-day, when everything is in transition, the multiplicity of thought and feeling is especially great.

It is impossible for me to define my own attitude with regard to the various Asian interpretations and evaluations. What matters above all is to listen, really to listen earnestly to what others are saying. This makes it necessary to put up calmly with criticisms both justified and unjustified, with views favourable and unfavourable alike, and to stand by our own beliefs. Finally, our space is too limited to raze the mountains of prejudice and to correct the numerous wrong opinions which we shall meet. I propose to show what Asians think of Western Christianity in general, and of the Churches, Church organization, Christian teaching, forms of devotion, morals, customs, art and Western Christian missions in particular. Finally, I shall give a critical evaluation of Asian views and the effects they have had.

CHAPTER ONE

HOW CHRISTIANITY IS SEEN AND JUDGED

In Asia we frequently hear and read that Christianity is equalled or surpassed by other religions, and is consequently by no means the supreme and absolute religion. What the West usually quotes as sign and evidence of the superior character of Christianity, as for instance the miracles of Christ and his saints, in most cases matters little to Asians. "We, too, have such miracles", they will say. "We even have greater ones. Buddha worked and lived such miracles as would make all Christian miracles look very insignificant indeed." The famous Kublai Khan made his conversion dependent on the Pope sending him men endowed, like pagan miracle workers, with miraculous powers. In Japan I heard of astonishing miracles performed by Buddhist monks in our day. Even a reference to Christian morality is not convincing. We talk with pride of the commandment to love our enemies; but a Chinese told me that this, too, existed in Asia. In his country people were used to say: "If I return good for evil, then my heart expands." In the Tao-te-king we find

1

the words: "Return kindness for enmity." Hindus, who before the Second World War made a study of Europe, remarked afterwards that Europeans were still moving along the periphery of religion. We had not yet reached its centre. According to Buddhists, Gautama's religion, by virtue of its spirituality, is vastly superior to the Christian faith.

The Koran recognizes Christ as a true prophet and Christianity as a genuinely revealed religion, a "religion of men of the book – Ahl al-Kitab".[1] It is granted that God made a covenant with Christians, and that the Christian faith may bring salvation. Christianity was founded by a genuine prophet, Christ; but it is not the highest religion. On the contrary, the original pure religion was deprived of its purity and sublimity by Jewish and Christian teachers. Paul, for example, spoilt the doctrine of Jesus. The doctrine of the Trinity implies the worship of three Gods. The doctrine of the Incarnation is a blasphemous insult to the transcendence of God. Jesus is not God. The pure original teaching was restored by Mohammed. Islam is the last, the most perfect religion, which was promised by Christ. In our time Moslems usually prove the supremacy of their faith in the following way: The rapid and

[1] See G. Vajda, "Ahl al-Kitab", in *Enc Isl,* i (Leiden and London, 1956), pp. 264–6.

complete victory of Islam in the world, especially in Palestine, Syria, Asia Minor and North Africa, that is, in parts that used to form the solid core of Christianity, can be explained solely through divine intervention; thus we are faced with a miracle which is proof of the superiority of Islam to Christianity. Islam has conquered large Christian countries; no Moslem country has yet been won by the Christian faith. Even modern Moslems, whose thought and actions are ruled by Christian influences, will value Islam more highly than Christianity. According to Mohammed Abduh (1849–1905), the founder of Egyptian Modernism, which is still of importance, Islam surpasses the Christian faith by virtue of its rationalism, its sense of reality and its renunciation of unattainable ideals.[2]

Moreover, Christianity is even accused of grave defects and errors and not infrequently altogether condemned. Even before the victory of Communism, the anti-Christian younger generation of China used to say that Christianity was a danger to their country; for, they maintained, it strangles reason, suppresses science, progress, liberty and

[2] R. Siraj ud Din, who was a convert from Islam to Christianity remarked, "The teaching of our Lord is admired (by the Moslems), even though they say it is too lofty to be practical". "The Vital Forces of Christianity and Islam", *IRM,* 2, (1913), p. 107.

human dignity and, by concentrating on a world beyond, leads to resignation and apathy and not towards a positive attitude towards life and the world. Christianity creates the inquisition, corruption and a slavish spirit. Tang Liang Li in his book *China in Revolt* wrote: "Young China is determined to put an end to the attempt of the Christian missions to dominate China's spiritual life. For they are convinced that Christianity in its decay, has nothing to offer to thoughtful people – clergy or lay – even in the West; since it is morally defective, intellectually absurd and historically untrue, it is not a suitable religion for the awakening Chinese who are certainly not a nation of savages! The enlightened West still believes in Joshua miraculously changing the sun in its course, and in the Immaculate Conception. Young China, on the contrary, is no longer prepared to be nourished by an inferior philosophy, by impracticable ethics, by the foolish superstitions and myths of the old world which are passed off by the majority of missionaries in China as divine revelation and historical truth."

Meanwhile the attacks on Christianity have become more frequent, vociferous and intense. In China and many other parts they surpass everything that has gone before. Christianity is branded as nonsense, folly, an obstacle to progress; it is opium for the people, the People's enemy

4

Number One. It is said to prevent the people from reaching paradise. Some, however, have expressed appreciation, assent and praise.

Nor is Europe condemned in all respects. Rabindranath Tagore was a severe critic of the West, but he also knew a Europe that is "great and good".[3] Art, literature, science, the fight against misery and want. "In the very heart of Europe there flows the purest stream of human kindness, love of justice and the readiness to make sacrifices for higher ideals. Centuries of Christian civilization have penetrated to its very core."[4] All this is evidence, he continued "that the fountains of eternal life in Europe are not dried up, and its rebirth will always come from there".[5] "In spite of its dislike, the East had the instinctive feeling that there is much to be learnt from the West, not only as regards the material means of its power but also the inner sources that are part of the spirit and the moral nature of Man."[6]

The case for Christianity is similar. In all spheres and among all nations of Asia we find people who appreciate and respect Christianity and adhere to it. These Asians are

[3] R. Tagore, *Nationalismus,* p. 112.
[4] Ibid., p. 83.
[5] Ibid., p. 84.
[6] Ibid., p. 194.

well-aware of the sins and shortcomings of Christians; but they believe that Christ's teaching is the true religion, and that Christians have the right end in view. Many Asians prefer the tenets and aims, the ideals and the saints of Christianity to all others. Many thousands of Japanese, Koreans, Chinese and Indochinese have gladly laid down their lives for Christ and his Church, in the firm belief that Christ is the way, the truth and the life, that he has brought peace and stilled the longing of the soul which is in harmony with his teaching, and that Christianity means communion with God. The fact that the Catholic Church in Japan endured centuries of persecution, without missionaries, without churches, is as significant as the wonderful beginnings of Christianity in Korea and the attitude of Christians in Vietnam. "Nothing human can be greater than Confucianism, Buddhism and Taoism. But Christianity is divine. It is a mistake to regard Christianity as Western. The West may be Christian (I wish it were more so), but Christianity is not Western. It is beyond East and West, beyond the old and the new. It is older than the old, newer than the new. It is more native to me than Confucianism, Taoism and Buddhism in whose milieu I was born. . . . It is no more true than the truth to say ever since I became a Catholic, my life has been a continued feast, a feast that satisfies without satiating. Adversities and tribulations there are a plenty, but even these are sweet, or rather they serve to bring out the marvellous sweetness of God. . . . Have I lost anything by being a Catholic? Absolutely nothing. On the contrary, I have gained Christ, and in gaining Christ I have gained all." Thus writes John Wu in *Beyond East and West*.

It is true that Christians are still very few in number. Most Asians remain non-Christians. But the situation may change. In many countries, even in Japan, people in all walks of life are moving towards Christianity. As long as there was no genuine religious freedom, on account of the religious policy of the government, the Japanese stayed aloof from Christianity. But since the war Shinto has lost its power. The Japanese people enjoy complete religious freedom. They are more susceptible to the Christian message, and conversions are more numerous.

Christianity has a strong and far-reaching influence beyond its boundaries. It represents an important factor in the spiritual and moral sphere. The Indian writer J. C. Ghose described Christianity as "the noblest and most progressive religion of our time". The Arya Samaj, the Aryan League of India, has little liking for Christianity. They regard the ancient Veda religion as the full and eternal truth which must be restored to its original purity. Yet in their teaching, cult, pastoral methods, in their dealings with the poor and oppressed as well as in their civilization they have adopted a great many practices from Christianity or have been stimulated by it. They seem to share the fate of the Prophet Balaam who went out to curse God's people but ended by blessing them. Other communities present similar features.

European Christianity does not only meet with hostility. On the contrary, its friends are to be found all over the world. Asian Christians, who on the whole are not much in favour of adapting the Christian faith to their Asian environment, since they do not wish to be reminded of the past and of their previous life, are particularly attached to European Christianity, even more so than far-seeing missionaries would like.

The Truth of Christianity

The opinion that Christianity is not the true religion is extremely widespread and significant. With its many "errors", its lack of unity and its undeniable "failures", it is argued, Christianity cannot possibly be the true religion. Later we shall deal with the "errors". Let us first consider its disunity and its "failures".

From hearsay, from the press and from their own experiences Asians are only too well-aware of the essential lack of unity in Christendom. With the exception of

Russia, of the Arab countries, of Afghanistan, Nepal, Bhutan and Tibet there is scarcely a territory or even a larger township in Asia without its missions of various Christian denominations, all fighting against each other. The consequences are evident. It is impossible, Asians will say, that a religion with so many different doctrines, customs, orders, and organizations can be the true faith. In any case, it would be difficult to discover the right denomination. If even Europeans cannot find their way about, how can Asians be expected to discover theirs? Especially in the mission field it soon becomes manifest how much depends upon the unity and upon the visible shape of the Church. How can we possibly convince Asians of the truth of our faith if we ourselves are not agreed on the true doctrine? How can we possibly convince them of the strength of our beliefs if we are incapable of overcoming our lack of unity? How can we unite men and nations if we cannot bridge our own divisions?

Our "failures", moreover, play an important part in Asian arguments. In the eyes of many, success is a proof of the truth and value of a cause; the masses, at any rate, are most strongly influenced by success. The man in the street believes that success is the sign of the justice of a cause. God is on the side of the conqueror: he wants him to rule. When Islam defeated Christianity in Western

Asia and North Africa, many Christians concluded: Islam must be willed by God, hence we must accept it. On the other hand, the Byzantines felt entitled to overthrow any emperor who was unsuccessful in his struggle against pagans and Moslems. Any Emperor of China incapable of protecting his people from want and misery forfeited his right to the throne. In Japan Christianity was rejected by great numbers for the simple reason that it was prohibited by the State and persecuted: what the State does not wish, cannot be genuine. Christianity, to this way of thinking, cannot be the true faith if in its own domain and in the mission field it achieves little or nothing. We shall refer later to this kind of argument and examine it more closely.

But not only the truth of European Christianity in general, its Christian character is being disputed.

Many Asian non-Christians hold Christ in high esteem and give him room in their hearts and in their places of worship.[7] There are many who admire, praise and love him. The Brahmin Keshub Chandra Sen, one time leader of the Brahmo-Samaj, had this to say about Christ: "This unique character, in the fulness of his self-sacrifice, presents the most touching miracle in world

[7] See A. Krämer, *Christus und Christentum im Denken des modernen Hinduismus* (Bonn, 1958); A. C. Underwood, *Contemporary Thought of India* (London, 1930), pp. 146–8.

history that I have witnessed and that the human spirit is capable of grasping. . . . This God-Man . . . proceeds daily across this vast peninsula . . . enlightening and healing the millions. He is a powerful reality in Indian history."[8] "There has, since the birth of Creation, been only one perfect man. This was Jesus. He was perfect because he was divine." As distinguished a writer as Narayan Vaman Tilak composed hymns to Christ. An Indian painter remarked, "Christ is the great idea of Hinduism. No Hindu can afford to ignore Christ; no Hindu can afford not to love Christ. We know Christ, our own Asiatic Christ, in his own natural colour".[9] A. M. Fairbairn was right in saying, "Christ is the only name the West has carried into the East, which the East received and praised and loved with sincerity and without qualification".[10] According to my own experiences in India, many Hindus own and study copies of the Bible and of the Imitation of Christ, and in various Hindu temples images of Christ are to be found on the walls. Dr. Sen, president of the Brahmo-Samaj of Patna on the Ganges, answered my question concerning India's attitude to Christ in the following way: "Christ is

[8] Fr. Heiler, *Christlicher Glaube und indisches Geistesleben,* p. 14. See H. W. Schomerus, *Indien und das Christentum,* ii, pp. 158–60.

[9] O. Buck, *Our Asiatic Christ,* 1.

[10] Ibid., vii. In Sri Aurobindos' book, *The Life Divine* (1951), though the name of Jesus is not mentioned.

in all our hearts. You cannot imagine how deeply Christ has penetrated our lives." A book recently published by Bhai Manilal C. Parekh, *A Hindu's Portrait of Jesus Christ* (Rajkot, 1953), offers a profound study of Jesus Christ and shows great love for his person. The author calls it, "My most humble tribute to Jesus Christ, whose 'Hindu disciple' I have been for the last forty years".

Buddhists, too, show understanding and respect for Christ. A leading Japanese Buddhist wrote that Christ is conceived by Buddhists also as a manifestation of the *dharmakaya* in a human form.[11] In the Himalayas, I found a picture of Christ even in a Lamaist monastery.

The Koran[12] sees in "Isa", the "Son of Maryam" one "in close touch with Allah", a prophet, a messenger of God, a miracle worker. The eighth article of the oldest Mohammedan Creed, attributed to Abu Hanifa, runs: "He who believes all that he is bound to believe, yet says: 'I do not know whether Moses and Jesus / Peace be with

[11] D. T. Suzuki, *Outlines of Mahayana-Buddhism* (London, 1907), p. 259. Buddhists hold similar opinions of other religious leaders; p. 261: "It will be evident from this that Buddhists are ready to consider all religious and moral leaders of mankind, whatever their nationality, as the Body of Transformation of the Dharmakaya"; p. 275: Even those doctrines and their authors that are apparently against the teachings of Buddhism are tolerated!

[12] For the position of Jesus in Islam, see D. B. Macdonald, "Isa" in *Enc Isl,* pp. 173–5.

them / are among the messengers – is an infidel."[13] The Moslem people in general respect the Gospels. Jesus and Mary "are held in the highest reverence by Moslems, who follow the teachings of the Koran".[14]

The position of European Christianity is entirely different. The overwhelming majority have little sympathy for it. It has, we are told, little or nothing to do with Christ. In the opinion of many Asians, Europe has long lost all real understanding of Christ and his teaching; the essence of Christianity has been watered down. It is not taken seriously; Europe no longer accepts the radicalism of the Bible; it completely lacks the revolutionary fervour of genuine Christianity. Over and over again Asians will repeat: Europe has betrayed Christianity, its most sacred possession.

Indians will argue that it was fatal for Christianity to have progressed towards the West – Rome-wards – with its essentially different, unspiritual, worldly, materialistic and militaristic character – before gaining ground in the spiritually congenial East. The West, they say, did not understand Christianity. So it became superficial. Christianity is thus merely a distortion of the original, genuine faith. The West endeavours to find the Kingdom of God

[13] *Enc Isl,* p. 33.
[14] Hassan Suhrawardy, *World Religions* (London).

in externals, and seeks to establish it by means of civilization and universal world renewal. Gandhi remarked in 1920: "I am firmly convinced that present-day Europe does not realize the spirit of God and Christianity, but the spirit of Satan. And Satan is most successful when he appears with the name of God on his lips. To-day Europe is Christian only in name. In reality it worships Mammon . . . I maintain that European Christianity is a denial of the Christianity of Christ. I cannot believe that, if Christ appeared in our midst, he would recognize the contemporary Christian churches, their liturgy, and their clergy." According to Rabindranath Tagore and others the West never had a real understanding of Christianity.[15]

Similar opinions are expressed in the Far East. Huh Shih and Lin Yutang have emphasized that Christians never learned to disobey as citizens and to follow Christ's commandment.[16]

[15] Sundhar Singh: "Gandhi and Tagore would have become Christians had they never visited Europe." Sayings of Sundhar Singh while in Switzerland. The Lausanne and Neufchatel Engl. Mag. 1922. Quoted from Fr. Heiler, *Sadhu Sundhar Singh*, p. 267. – At the Stockholm Christian World Conference in 1925 Paul Althaus said about the Orientals: "They do not measure the Gospels against Europe but condemn Europe by Gospel standards." *The Stockholm World Conference. Official Report*, (1926), p. 378.

[16] Huh Shih and Lin Yutang, *China's Own Critics*, p. 101.

Christians, too, agree with such criticism. The Eastern national churches claim to have preserved original Christianity better than Rome and the Protestant churches of the West. All these Churches had refashioned Christianity in accordance with their own spirit and European character. Farther East the criticism is still more trenchant. Uchimura, a well-known Japanese Protestant, told the German ambassador Dr. Solf, as the latter repeated to me in Tokyo – the Japanese welcomed Christianity as taught by Christ. For it stemmed from the East, and with its parables and many other features was well adapted to the Japanese. But unfortunately Christianity had become dogmatic and clerical. This type of Christianity they must reject.

Sadhu Sundar Singh visited Europe repeatedly and in the end turned his back on it in disappointment. There are, he said, true Christians in Europe, but not all Europeans are Christians. In Europe he had found a worse type of paganism than in pagan countries. It was true that there people worship idols. But Europeans worshipped their own selves which was much worse. "I began to realize that no European country can be regarded as Christian, and that everywhere there are only a few individual Christians." The Christian religion was not to be blamed for this, he maintained, just as Christ was not to be blamed for conditions in Palestine. "One day I was sitting on the

15

bank of a river in the Himalayas: from the water I lifted a lovely stone, round and hard, and smashed it. Its inside was completely dry. The stone had been in the water for a long time, but the water had not penetrated into it. It is just the same with people in Europe: for centuries they have been surrounded by Christianity, they have been totally immersed in its blessings; they live within Christianity, but Christianity has not entered their inner being and has not come to life within them. Yet the fault lies not in Christianity, but in their own hardness of heart. Materialism and intellectualism have hardened their hearts. Therefore I am not astonished that many people in those parts cannot understand Christ."

To this criticism he added: If Europe, which gained the whole world but forfeited its soul and is now in a desperate plight, desires to meet genuine Christianity, it will have to learn from Asia. *Ex Oriente lux!* The East is the life-giver, the mother of all religions. All men must return to it. It is the mission of the East to bring the light of the Gospel and true Christianity to Europe. In the view of Sadhu Sundar Singh and others the time would come when Indian missionaries would preach the Gospel in the West.

Asian opinion has been confirmed by declarations from Europeans. K. Saunders wrote that owing to their natural disposition and their nutrition Asia's millions are much closer than Europeans to the Sermon of the Mount. J. Ch. Winslow was convinced that the West needs India for its spiritual development. We are arriving at an ever deeper understanding, he wrote, that the light from India's religious genius, as reflected upon Christian life and thought, is of an almost revolutionary character, and that it will show up our own understanding of Christianity as being quite inadequate.[17] The Anglican Bishop Westcott declared that we would not arrive at a proper appreciation of the Gospel of St. John before India had become Christian.[18] Friso Melzer wrote: "Whoever has looked beyond the boundaries of his own denomination and met other forms of Christian living, can never expect Johannean Christianity to arise among the Western nations, but solely in the East." Baron von Hügel asked: "Where else, if not in India, will the unique nature and power of Christianity have as fine a chance of being understood?"

These remarks raise very serious problems. Are the Asians right? Are we still Christians? Have we ever been Christians? Fedor Stepun wrote: "It is no mere coincidence that hitherto all ideas that changed the fate of the world have had to pay for their victory with a certain loss of

[17] J. Winslow, *The Indian Mystics* (London, 1926), p. 8.
[18] J. C. Winslow, *Christian Yoga or the Threefold Path of Union with God* (London, 1923), p. 4.

3*

their substance. Even the history of European Christianity is largely a history of Christendom betraying Christianity. Who could doubt that this very betrayal lies at the heart of the immeasurable sufferings through which we have to pass to-day." It is the teaching of the Catholic Church that she has preserved the substance of Christ's Gospel and his redemptive work faithfully and without adulteration. But she does not deny that many among the faithful neither understood nor followed him.

We meet with the allegation that Christianity is lacking in truly Christian elements especially in the version that Christianity is a typically *European* religion. Everything about it is more or less European: its cast of thought and doctrine, propagation and theology, liturgy and piety, the ministry and missionary efforts, the structure of its communities and ways of expression, language and music, architecture and painting, sculpture and vestments. In this connection the Protestant denominations are the first to come to mind since they show the distinct imprint of their founders and the countries of their origin and are to a large extent "national churches"; however the same applies to the "Roman" Catholic Church which, for instance, according to Sadhu Sundar Singh, is only one expression, one facet of the development of the races and civilizations of Europe.

The conclusions drawn from these opinions are known. As a European or "alien" religion Christianity has no message for the East unless it adapts itself to the Oriental mind. A persistent struggle against undue foreign influence and Westernization is going on. The austere forms of Western piety are, as Parekh remarks, not suited to the Hindu with his spirituality, his power of imagination, the ardour of his faith, his religious enthusiasm and contemplative nature. Similar comments from other nations could be quoted.

In answer to this criticism we can argue that Christianity is not a Western religion. For a long time many missionaries favoured Western ways of thought and worship. In many parts of Asia our religion appears somewhat Western, but this need not be. After all, Christianity in India is almost as old as Christianity itself, and for a long time there were no European influences at work there.

Value-Judgements

The criticisms quoted above already imply value-judgements; they can be supplemented by others.

Not a few Asians believe that Western Christianity can be easily disposed of as "historicism". Our faith is founded on historical facts. Revelation is history. Unlike the avataras or descents to earth of the Indian deities, the

Incarnation of Our Lord is an unique, unrepeatable historical event. Christ, at a certain moment in time, founded his Church, and he will return at a given moment. In many non-Christian faiths there are products of the imagination rather than historical facts. The Greeks, too, did not always clearly distinguish between what was purely "internally visualized and thought" and actual facts and events. When I asked a Japanese professor of philosophy in Tokyo whether the Japanese seriously believed in the existence of Kwanon the "goddess of mercy", he replied this was not a question a Japanese would ask. For most Asians things in themselves are not so important as the feelings they arouse. The experience of Christ within us is more significant than the Christ who lived two thousand years ago.

The widest gap separates Christians from the Hindus and those akin to them in mind,[19] who are not interested in or even hostile to history, who see in it mere fluctuations, transience, eternal change and non-existence; to them the only realities are meta-historical and metaphysical. "The consciousness of the Hindus is the most thoroughly anti-historical of all types of consciousness in the world",

[19] It is significant that the Indians possess no biographies of the Buddha; on the whole they know very little about him, but all the more about his teaching.

wrote Berdyaev. "All that was most profound in India was not connected with history; there was no genuine history, ... no genuine historical process." "The eternal empirical world" is "the lower reality", "the lower order of things which must be overcome, and which we have to renounce in order to enter the metaphysical truth that bears the seal of the spirit." Many Hindu sayings can only be understood when we keep this attitude in mind.

Its very age is another argument against Christianity. Moslems believe they can settle the case against Christianity by saying that their own religion is the latest and youngest. Christianity, on the other hand, is ancient and only a first step on the path leading to the faith of the Prophet. Other accusations strike more deeply. Our Christianity, it is said, is not only old but also obsolete, senile and petrified. According to Rabindranath Tagore, Pride in her traditions has hardened Europe's heart.[20] "Europe has become incapable of giving to the East what is best in her, and of accepting in a right spirit the wisdom that the East has stored for centuries".[21] Europe and Christianity are here identical concepts.

Formerly, by virtue of its connection with European civilization, Christianity was regarded in Asia as a religion

[20] R. Tagore, *Nationalismus,* p. 129.
[21] Ibid., p. 129.

21

both mature and of youthful vigour. Christianity and modern civilization seemed to be essentially and inseparably joined together. Whoever aspired to the latter would also have to accept the former. In many cases this argument was responsible for the conversion especially of progressive-minded people. Nowadays, however, Christianity and European civilization are separated: there is no connection between them: you can have one without the other, you ought even to accept European civilization without Christianity, for Christianity is held to be a relic from the Middle Ages that does not fit into the modern world; even in Europe it is said to be out of date.

Christianity or the Church are supposed to be obsolete in yet another sense. A Japanese Catholic once wrote to me that nothing new of any importance had arisen in our Church. We had only to look at the "modern Churches", their dogmatism, exegesis and Church history. In answer to these and similar accusations we are bound to emphasize that the Church, by her very nature, must in many and essential respects remain unchanged. It is for us to accept her truth and fashion our lives accordingly. But up to a point this Japanese friend may well be right. With regard to church architecture, for instance, we have recently witnessed a period of decline. We have exhausted ourselves in historicism, and even where we have experimented with new forms, we have created nothing really worthwhile. Theology has become mere rethinking and restating of what was thought and said before. Only rarely does anyone say anything unconventional and new. In order to avoid giving offence and incurring danger, certain problems have been eschewed, and antiquated methods and formulae adhered to. Christianity needs creative artists who, though well aware of the tradition of the Church, blaze new trails; it needs theologians who from Holy Scriptures and tradition draw forth not only *vetera* but also *nova;* it needs men who in spite of all dangers seek new ways in both doctrine and life; it needs believers who combine loyalty to divine tradition with a mind open to the words, working, and demands of the Holy Spirit in this our day, *quae temporis dei sunt.*

Age and senility, however, are not the only accusations raised against Christianity, but also their opposite – novelty. Most non-Christian religions of Asia are of greater age, and are proud of it. As a new and young religion, Christianity cannot be considered by the followers of Asian religions, the more so as it has nothing fresh to offer. The argument runs: "Away with the emissaries from the West. What little good they may bring, we knew a thousand years ago." The Superior of the Buddhist monastery Djung Dju-sen in Tsinanfu declared:

"We look upon Christianity as a religion younger than ours. We do not take it into account."

The right answer to such remarks is to be found in the *Retractationes* (I, xiii, 3) of St. Augustine:

"What is called Christianity to-day has always existed in the past, and was never unknown since the beginnings of mankind until Christ appeared in the flesh. . . ." There is also a passage by John Henry Newman: "Christianity is only the continuation and conclusion of what professes to be an earlier revelation, which may be traced back into prehistoric times, till it is lost in the darkness that hangs over them."[22] Moreover, it can be argued that novelty in itself is not a sign that a thing is wrong or worthless. Only those who know nothing about it can maintain that the Christian religion possesses no values that are unknown to other religions.

There is very little understanding of the intolerance shown by Christianity. Asians are used to seeing their religions, especially Brahmanism, Hinduism, Buddhism and Islam, divided into many factions. In Hinduism we find Vishnuism, Shivaism and innumerable other schools of thought. In Japanese Buddhism there are eight principal

[22] J. H. Newman, *An Essay in Aid of a Grammar of Assent* (London, 1939), p. 431.

sects, each again subdivided into smaller groups, the Nichiren-shu, for instance, into eight or nine. Unity and harmony do not exist even within each individual sect. Among the Zen masters there are, according to Daisetz Teitaro Suzuki, "such contrasts that they might cause confusion. What the one affirms, the other will flatly deny". A great many Asians consider a diversity of religions and denominations as sensible and useful, even necessary. Not all religions of the world are, of course, equally good and equally perfect. Yet each of them corresponds to some natural trend, cast of thought, and phase of need and development. Each of them has at least a preparatory value. Even the least perfect religion has a mission of its own: as an introduction and preparation for the true faith.

A Chinese catechumen told me he thought it impossible that a certain make of stockings which had been bought and worn for decades could be quite without value. It is much the same with religions, he said. If untold numbers of people had for centuries found contentment and happiness in Buddhism, surely there must be something in it. The Japanese have a proverb: "Every road leads to its end. Every religion is good. Do not various roads lead up to Mt. Fuji?" Junyu Kitayama asked: "Is the Kingdom of God really so monotonous and so poor that it can manifest itself only in one single religion and way of life?"

Buddhists believe in reincarnation and the "gradual progress of the individual towards the Divine Light". Everyone lives in the state which corresponds to the karma of his previous life and will, in his next existence, attain to that reincarnation which conforms to his present way of life. The present life is not the only one and does not determine our eternal destiny. Hence the tolerance of Buddhists towards all forms of religion.

Hinduism is characterized by a similar attitude. All religions are justified and good – with the exception of those that claim exclusiveness. Ramakrishna said: "Just as we may climb the roof of a house by way of a ladder or a bamboo pole, or by using a staircase or a rope, so there are different ways and means of reaching God, and every religion in the world demonstrates one of these ways." Vivekananda maintains that all religions are true. Their colours are different, yet all these colours taken together give you white, the colour of love. All religions possess but parts of truth. According to Rabindranath Tagore, religion is a matter of experience; everyone must have his own religion. "In death what is manifold becomes one; in life what is one becomes manifold." "There will be *one* religion only when God is dead." In Radhakrishnan's opinion it is not unnatural for different people to have different religions. He and others regard it as a question of taste and temperament.

Tolerance is not alien even to Islam.[23] As Averroes says, one and the same truth can be presented in different ways. Many Moslems, especially Sufis, have similar ideas. The Ismailis, or "Sect of the Seven", teach that for the "Gnostic" all religions are equally true and equally false. Only God is one because he is all, and each form of life is only one facet of his being.

Tolerance, as shown by the examples of Averroes and similarly of Shankara and Akbar, is not a characteristic of second- and third-rate minds but, on the contrary, of the greatest and most famous sages of Asia.

Vast numbers of Asians even believe that the individual can adhere to different religions at the same time; many, in fact, do so. It is therefore impossible to compile satisfactory religious statistics for the Far East. In the West we say "either – or", "Catholic *or* Protestant", in the East we have "as well as": "Shintoist *and* Buddhist". We like clear distinctions, Asians prefer conciliation and compromise.[24]

[23] See Koran, Sure ii, p. 257: "There must be no coercion in religion".

[24] Compare this with what Goethe wrote on January 6, 1813 in a letter to Friedrich Heinrich Jacobi: "In view of the manifold elements of my nature, I cannot be satisfied with *one* way of thinking; as a poet and artist I am a polytheist; on the other hand, as a man of

27

As P. K. Mok, a Chinese student, put it: "The spirit of the West does not seem able to comprehend how a good and pious man can at the same time be a Confucian, a Buddhist, a Taoist and a Christian. European Christians believe this to be wrong and impossible; but thousands of Chinese Christians live it." A Chinese will worship Confucius to-day, Buddha to-morrow and Taoist deities the day after. It all depends on circumstances, what best suits his needs and frame of mind at a particular time. In the last resort Confucianism, Taoism and Buddhism are for him only *one* religion. A Chinese factory manager in Hongkong told me once that he everywhere conformed to the religion of the country; thus in China he lived as a follower of Confucius or Buddha, in America as a Christian.[25]

science, a pantheist, and the one quite as decidedly as the other. If, as a moral being, I require a God for my personality, I can find one. Things celestial and things terrestrial form so vast a realm that only the organs of all creatures together are able to grasp it."

[25] The spiritual situation is described very strikingly by Pearl S. Buck, who remarked that "to the people one religion more or less did not make much difference. It was always possible that somewhere there existed an additional God hitherto unknown to them, and it might be advisable to be in his good books even though he might be the white man's God" (*Gottesstreiter im fernen Land*, Berlin 1937, p. 133). "A hostile attitude made itself felt only when Andrew (a Protestant missionary) boldly announced that his God was the only true God" (p. 134). A Chinese priest thought that everyone has a God of his own, who to him is the true God, "and there are enough for all of us".

On joyful occasions the Japanese are Shintoists, on mournful ones Buddhists. "The Shinto deities", wrote K. Florenz, "are connected with good fortune, Buddha, however, with the afflictions of life, and with death." Almost all the Japanese have two altars or shrines in their homes, one dedicated to the Shintoist Kami, the other to the Buddhist Hotoke. It may happen, as the Vicar General of Kobe, Mgr. Fage, and others have told me, that Buddhists and Shintoists will pray inside or in front of a Catholic Church.[26] The Mongol Khans of the Middle Ages remained loyal to their faith, in spite of all attempts at conversion, yet participated in Catholic services and asked Catholic missionaries for their blessing.

That is not the whole story. The religions themselves are not isolated, they are frequently mixed. Nearly all of them are inclined towards syncretism, even Islam

---

[26] Kaibara Ekiken (1630–1714), one of the most important and most influential philosophers in Japan, adhered to Monism, a creed that knows of no life after death, but at the same time he definitely subscribed to the national Shinto cult which admits it. O. Graf, in his valuable biography of this man, adds: "The average Japanese regards even to-day a clarification of the question, whether the cult of the 'Kami' . . . is compatible with other views of life, as quite superfluous." O. Graf, *Kaibara Ekiken* (Leiden, 1942), p. 12. P. Byrne told me in Otsu that a Buddhist made a donation of no less than 600 yen for his altar with the comment: "I think it is a privilege to help in making a home for God."

which was already in its beginnings the product of a combination of religions. In these matters compromise is regarded not only as possible and permissible but even as beneficial and necessary. Men and nations who have the courage to combine heterogeneous elements are admired and praised. Masaharu Anesaki, for instance, proudly speaks of the "special Japanese genius for the conciliation of opposites".[27] Frequently syncretism assumes forms which seem really incredible. There are religions the syncretism of which includes even the most heterogeneous and basest practices. The sacred scriptures of the Hindu include the Upanishads, with their radical negation of the world and of life, as well as the Veda with their positive attitude to both.[28] A Hindu may be a polytheist, monotheist, theopanist or atheist. Auguste Barth wrote of Hinduism, "Même sa diversité est l'essence" — "What it does not include, does not exist at all". Hinduism excludes nothing; it embraces all things. But that is not all. Frequent attempts have been made in Asia to unite the different Asian religions. Akbar (d. 1605), the great ruler

[27] M. Anesaki, *Religious Life of the Japanese People,* p. 51.

[28] In the famous Bhagavadgita, ideas from both the Vedanta and the Sankhya are expounded. The Vedanta is monistic-idealistic, the Sankhya doctrine is atheist-dualistic. The author or editor combined both.

of the Mongol Empire, who broke away from Islam, proclaimed the eclectic *'Tawhid-i-ilahi'* in which the common features of the religions which he had studied were merged. Similarly dozens of reformers have tried to combine the allegedly genuine and valuable elements of a diversity of religions. We may call to mind the many new religions arising in Japan and Korea.[29]

It seems to us that the doctrine of the truth, value and justification of all religions is fundamentally identical with the belief that no single religion could be true and perfect. Many Asians draw the same conclusions. All religions are only potentialities. Therefore none must rise above the others, Christianity not excepted.

The idea of the fundamental kinship of all religions is also widespread. At one time it was the fashion in the West to discover in all religions parallel and comparable phenomena, and to discern in them the true nature, the quintessence of religion: the true, the good and the divine. Hence in these circles all missionary activity was regarded as superfluous. Similar ideas are still prevalent in Asia.

---

[29] For many Asians tolerance is linked with their conception of God. You can talk and negotiate with the deities of the non-Christians, indistinct figures as they may be, whereas the God of the Christians is a zealot (see 2 Cor 11:2; Deut. 32:16). The heathen worship Gods who correspond to them, but the Christians a God who will contradict them often in the harshest manner.

31

The one religion is embodied in historically conditioned individual forms. All religions are variations on the same theme. Each has an eternal, timeless substance of its own and in this it is in harmony with the others. According to Rabindranath Tagore, "all religions are essentially alike; they differ only in their forms, like water, which though the same everywhere, is bordered by various shores and allotted to different nations". "Fundamentally", Tagore wrote, "Christ preached exactly the same message as Buddha." In Seishin (Korea) a Russian told me of a Japanese maid-servant in the house of one of his relatives, who insisted on the children worshipping God in their Russian-orthodox way whereas she kept her own faith. She said in explanation: "Religion is the same everywhere, but the Churches vary according to different countries." The Zen-master Joka wrote these lines:

> One moon, and one only
> Is reflected in all waters.
> All moons in the water
> Are one with the One moon.

The following remark is attributed to the famous Prince Shotoku: "The religions of Japan are a tree with Shinto as its root, Confucianism as its stem and Buddhism as its foliage and blossoms."

In the opinion of many Asians, there is no basic difference between Christianity and other religions. In Seoul (Korea) I had a long conversation about Buddhism and Christianity with priests in a Buddhist monastery; at the end a Korean who had been listening in silence, exclaimed that Buddhism and Christianity were identical. Both religions had the same beliefs. The headmaster of a Japanese high school for girls, himself a follower of Jodo-Shinshu but married to a Catholic, once asked Fr. G. Gemeinder, a missionary of the Society of the Divine Word, to a religious disputation. "When he spoke", the priest wrote afterwards, "I was vividly reminded of our lectures on dogmatics, when we studied the doctrine of grace and the Greek Fathers. 'We are redeemed', he said, 'by repenting of our sins and by loving confidence in Amida, the infinite, supreme Being.' 'Do you mean that in a pantheistic sense?' I asked. 'No, not at all. Man retains his personal existence but is permeated by the Divine.' I then explained to him our doctrine of grace, the supernatural rebirth of man or, in Eckhart's words, the birth of God within us. 'I really see no difference between your views and mine', he said." Gemeinder concludes: "After very careful examination I was able to admit that his conceptions both of God and of grace were completely Catholic." Certain circles deliberately set out to obliterate or at least minimize the differences between the non-Christian religions of Asia

4*

and Christianity. Hindus, for instance, like to think that Hinduism and Christianity, if properly understood, are fundamentally alike; you have but to remove the inessentials that have attached themselves to the real esoteric core of both religions in the course of centuries. Many quotations from the Bible in the religious literature of the East can but strengthen the impression that Vishnuism and Christianity preach and pursue the same ideas.

Many Asians, thoroughly relativistic in spiritual and religious matters as they are, are therefore prone to an easygoing complaisance, just as their personal conduct is determined by the ideals of adaptability and compliance. Hendrik Kraemer remarked of Hinduism: "Just as nature is not interested in truth, but in manifestation, in realizations, in shades, so Hinduism is not really interested in religious truth but in the endless possibilities of religious realization and expression".[30] Conditions in some other religions are not very different. Many Asians think it foolish to speak of one truth and one religion which is binding on all. Only the sage, the gnostic, and only he, will discover the true and absolute religion, which is a mystery. All others are only on their way to the goal. Similarly all religions are only approximations to the absolute. This

[30] H. Kraemer, *The Christian Message in a Non-Christian World,* p. 160 et seq.

relativism has been strengthened by modern spirituality which, while doing away with all absolutes, has fallen a prey to the pseudo-absolute.

In many places, especially in the Far East, relativism is connected with utilitarianism and pragmatism. Here the decisive factor is the tangible advantage of a thing, its practical usefulness, its creative force – not truth in itself.[31] The first question a Japanese will ask is invariably: "What is such and such a religion going to do about social questions such as the family, the State, the *kokutai* (the spiritual foundations of the State)?"[32] The Chinese may ask with equally brutal egoism: "What advantages will my conversion bring me?" Sometimes this pragmatism finds a very curious expression. A non-Christian said to a missionary who had expounded the true Faith: "You are right, but do give in – and there will be peace."

After this nobody will be astonished that Asians accuse us of dogmatic intolerance, and regard our teaching of the

[31] In Paltoku (Manchuria) I learned that pagans will frequently reply "Quite right" to our expounding of the Faith, but it does not occur to them to draw the evident conclusion.

[32] L. Paul, *Zweierlei Flamme,* p. 325. In the East pure research is not of much account. Utilization is of prime importance. No philosophy is pure philosophy, they are all doctrines of salvation. In this context it is significant that Fukuzawa Yukichi, the influential literary exponent of utilitarianism in nineteenth-century Japan, recommended the acceptance of Christianity for his country, though he personally rejected it.

35

absoluteness, universal validity and binding power of Christianity as unacceptable. Christ's claim to universal kingship, they say, shows arrogance and presumption. A Brahmin remarked to a Hindu acquaintance of mine: "In my opinion, Christ was a narrow-minded man. For he said: 'Go ye and teach all nations; he who does not believe will be damned'. Our faith tolerates everything." Gandhi regarded Christ as the greatest figure in world history, and Christianity the only road towards the solution of the Indian question, yet he did not become a Christian, partly because Jesus occupies such a unique and exclusive position in Christianity. "Christ", he remarked, "is *one* radiant revelation of God but not the only one." A Moslem wrote that he accepted the divine mission of Jesus and believed in his precepts. But "it was not in Jesus only that the Holy Spirit was made manifest." "God did not invent and reveal the Holy Spirit for Jesus alone."[33] We are here faced with what Wilhelm Dilthey called religious-universalistic theism, that is, a religion which, while believing in God, finds this God revealed not only in one religion, but in all outstanding philosophical and religious thinkers and even in every noble human being. There is a still greater outcry in non-theist circles against the Christian

[33] *IRM* (1937), p. 177 et seq. In Trichinopoly a Hindu told me he was a Christian if and as far as he need not be exclusively a Christian.

doctrine of revelation. Tai Hsü declares that the doctrine of Christ as the only perfect revelation of God makes no sense.

It is true that Christians, and Catholics in particular, are intolerant where dogmatic theology is concerned; and we consider relativism as mere hedging and a sign of lack of determination. A certain measure of intolerance is characteristic of every genuine dogmatic creed. A religion which abandons the doctrine of its absolute truth and uniqueness has surrendered its position and yields to indifferentism. Truth is indivisible and incompatible with error.

These truths meet with understanding in many parts of Asia. A fair number of Asians are convinced that *one* religion only can be the true faith which leads to salvation; many others appreciate the argument. Here I have in mind not only Moslems, but also followers of Far Eastern religions. The well-known Shinto scholar Hirata Atsutane (d. 1843) referred to the doctrine that all roads (the beliefs of Kami, Ju and Buddha) were identical. The adherents of this doctrine have songs like this:

> Rain, snow and ice
> Differ from one another.
> Yet once they have descended
> They become waters of the same stream.

Hirata Atsutane commented on this: "In order ... not to be deceived by this lie we must keep our eyes open and read the Scriptures." Toyohiko Kagawa, a Japanese Christian, wrote: "It may be said that although many paths lead upwards, it is the same moon we see from the summit. That is why we cannot understand that Jesus Christ should be our sole guide. Buddhism, Omoto, Tenri or Islam, all these religions are good. They all contain truth and guidance, but some of them will lead us farther than the sixth stage, others than the fourth, and still others tire and take a rest before even having passed the first stage. Some pause at the second stage, others reach only the third. Buddhism may take us as far as the ninth stage, but since it comes to a halt there, I myself choose not Buddhism, but Christianity, for I desire to climb to the very top."

Moreover, denial of the freedom of conscience meets with opposition. The Catholic Church knows and aims at the true freedom of conscience, the freedom to seek truth and goodness, freedom without physical compulsion; but she rejects the false freedom of conscience inherent in the doctrine of liberal autonomy.[34] Conscience is determined by truth. We cannot all be allowed to think, to

[34] *Denz*, 1690 and 1779.

speak and to act as we please according to our limited judgement. The Catholic Church bases her jurisdiction on the knowledge of the absolute truth of her teaching. At the same time she can point to the fatal results of a false freedom of conscience, which has contributed to the spiritual disintegration of the modern world.

The practical consequences of dogmatic intolerance, for example, the efforts to win the whole world and supplant all other religions, also have an unpleasant effect in Asia. All attempts "to make one's own religion dominant everywhere and at all times" are, according to Rabindranath Tagore, symptoms of sectarianism. "If ever such a catastrophe should befall mankind that it would be swallowed up by one single religion, God would have to provide another Noah's Ark in order to save his creatures from annihilation of the soul. . . ."

On the other hand, there are Asians who approve of our attitude. A Japanese Jesuit wrote to me: "A Japanese colleague told me: 'All judgement rests with God; our only aim should be to give others pleasure'. I absolutely reject this attitude. We must love God more than our fellow men. Whether a thing gives someone pleasure or not is not all that matters. The main concern is to work for the glory of God."

What Asians probably find most repulsive are the

attempts to propagate the Kingdom of God by purely secular means, for example, by Crusades, religious wars, persecutions and expulsions. Nobody can fail to recognize the disastrous results of such methods in Asia. The Crusades are one of the causes of Moslem antipathy to Christianity. An Apostolic Delegate in Africa and a Methodist missionary in India both declared that the repercussions of the Crusades are still in evidence. Nobody will expect the Turks, who throughout the ages were fought as the arch-enemies of Christianity, to have a special predilection for Christianity.

It is doubtful whether in practice the Christian peoples are as intolerant as Asians assume. However, the following facts are doubtlessly true: during the first three centuries Christians demanded religious freedom from the State; from Constantine the Great onward they received preferential treatment; after Theodosius the Great the Catholic faith held a monopoly; throughout the Middle Ages the Church exercised pressure upon the heathen[35] and had

[35] In such matters even a Saint like Gregory the Great was a man of his age. For, in hearing that there were still pagans in Sardinia, he wrote: "Nam si cuiuslibet episcopi in Sardinia insula paganum rusticum invenire potuero, in eodem episcopo fortiter vindicabo. Jam vero si rusticus tantae fuerit perfidiae et obstinationis inventus, ut ad Deum venire minime consentiat, tanto pensionis onere gravandus est, ut ipsa exactionis suae

heretics judged and punished – even with death – by the State; fanatical movements in the Middle Ages were cruelly persecuted. It is also true that force was used in the service of the Church, not only in the Crusades. Yet we must not overlook the fact that, for example, Islam was not only a religion but also a secular power, and that the Popes had to defend the West and could only save it from chaos by the use of force. Some of these attempts, it is true, must be regarded as tragically un-Christian. Even the Church has had to learn her lesson. To-day it is Catholic teaching that nobody may be compelled to accept the Faith.[36] The Catholic Church has always condemned that tolerance which means indifference to the truth and the approval of wrong convictions; but in the name of charity, she demands civic tolerance for people holding other faiths and considers respect for every honest conviction a moral duty.

Tolerance, after all, has not always been popular throughout Asia. Everyone is acquainted with the history of Islam and its violent methods. In Japan, right up to the end of the Second World War, there could be no question of genuine freedom of thought, faith and teaching. Woe upon anyone who attacked the dogma of the divinity of

poena compellatur ad rectitudinem festinare." *Mon. Germ.,* EE I, p. 261; *Greg. Ep.,* IV (May 26), p. 594.

[36] *CJC,* can. 1351.

the Emperor! The principle of tolerance proclaimed in the 1889 Constitution long remained a scrap of paper. In 1936, I was told in Japan of persecutions of Christians. The expert on China, Johann Jakob Maria de Groot,[37] showed how wrong travellers and writers were in praising the Chinese as a whole for their peace-loving and tolerant spirit. In the Emperor Yung-tcheng's commentaries on the "Sacred Edict" of the Emperor Kang-hsis we read: "Crush the heretics, just as if you were dealing with thieves and robbers, water or fire." It is unnecessary to point out that Chinese Communists are anything but tolerant. We need only think of enforced ideological instruction for priests and forced signatures, not to mention brain-washing. In Asia Christianity has had to endure many severe persecutions of long duration until recent times. In Burma and Siam, in China, Korea and Japan it has suffered more persecutions and produced more martyrs than in Europe. Even Buddhism did not remain completely untainted by intolerance and the urge to persecute. We have only to remember Nichiren and the Nichiren-shu in Japan. "The much-lauded tolerance of the Indians is a mere fairy tale. The Indian people are no more tolerant than other nations. In their history there is no lack of bloody per-

[37] J. J. M. de Groot, *Sectarianism and Religious Persecutions in China,* 2 vols. (Amsterdam, 1903).

secutions of other creeds."[38] A Brahmin in Trichinopoly related sadly that because of the hostile attitude of his relatives after his conversion, he would have been unable to live, but for the help of the Jesuit fathers. Hendrik Kraemer is right in suggesting that in this whole context we should not speak of "tolerance" but of "truth-equalitarianism" or "truth-indifferentism", that is, of apathy or indifference to the truth.[39]

Asian Christians, too, have complained of Western intolerance, of the lack of interest and respect shown by European missionaries and Christians who, they allege, aimed only at latinizing and westernizing Oriental Christianity. Here we have, in fact, made many mistakes. Even to-day, an indigenous Christianity of Latin features is fostered in Palestine. To this day, "Latin" and "Catholic" are likely to be identified. To this day many call Latin *the* language of the Church – as if there were no other liturgical languages. Not so very long ago Polish Catholics were guilty of oppressing the adherents of the Uniate rite in Poland. But the sins of individual Christian nations must not be laid at the door of the Church as a whole. The Catholic Church leaves no doubt that the Latin Church is only a part of the universal Church, and that her pale is

[38] H. W. Schomerus, *Indien und das Christentum,* ii, p. 104.
[39] H. Kraemer, *The Christian Message in a Non-Christian World,* p. 207.

not identical with it. Thus the *Codex Juris Canonici* is, of course, valid only for the Latin Church.[40]

Criticism of the "effeminate" character of Christianity is less frequent than that of its intolerance. However, we are told, Christianity is a religion for the weak. It is suitable only for them, not for the proud, vigorous and ambitious people of our time. The Japanese headmaster of a commercial college in North Korea told me that only men who were afraid would adopt the Christian faith. Really healthy and virile people did not consider it at all. Tai Hsü, a well-known Chinese Buddhist leader who had a great influence through his lectures, writings and schools, considered Christianity, because of its allegedly naive supernaturalism, to be a religion for feeble and superstitious natures. Nobody, he held, would be able to stand his ground in this world supported by a religion which banishes hatred, enjoins love of one's enemy and does not allow the faithful to resist evil. Prince Ito, the Japanese national hero, said: "To my mind religion is completely superfluous in the life of the nation. Science is far superior to superstition. What else is religion, Christianity no less than Buddhism, but superstition and a source of national weakness? As for myself, I am far from regretting the almost universal trend

[40] *CJC,* can. 1.

44

in Japan towards freethinking and atheism, since I cannot see how they should constitute a danger to society."

These are doubtless prejudices and errors of judgement. But they, too, contain a grain of truth. We have a habit of seeing Jesus above all as the mild and loving Saviour. We have only to look at the way he was described during the last century. We can hardly find anything but "the dear Lord", who as "a babe" lay in his "little crib", who talked about flowers and birds, fondled the little ones, loved the poor and was altogether charming. Can we be surprised that many pagans refuse to recognize his transcendence? How often do we preach of him who was "The Lord" though still in his crib (Luke 2:11); who caused his mother to suffer (Luke 2:48); who fought with the devil and drove the money-lenders from the temple with his scourge, who exposed the hypocrites, had deadly foes and persecutors and walked across the stormy sea?[41]

Christians have been inclined to represent Christianity, too, as a sweet and easy thing. Numerous Catholic devotions aim at bringing peace of mind, emotional satisfaction and gentle joys. When we compare many modern meditations on the Passion of Christ with the report in the Gospels, we find, on the one hand, a sober description

[41] See P. Angier, *Jésus, pierre de scandale* (Paris, 1955).

45

without any emotional appeal, on the other, nothing but sheer sentimentality. Some Sacred Heart devotions convey the impression that our Lord is perpetually in tears and needs human consolation. Yet in the beginning, Christianity was a virile religion. The sermons reported in the Acts of the Apostles are addressed to "men" and "brethren". None of the sermons is sentimental. In the New Testament, Christianity is a lucid and powerful religion.

Christianity is not only accused of catering for the needs of the weak and defenceless, it is also criticized for its inefficiency and impotence. The Christian nations of Europe show a deep gulf between religion and everyday life. Neither in economics nor in politics, we are told, has our Christianity proved a living force. The most convincing proof of this is the self-mutilation of Europe. Not a single vital question is radically and resolutely tackled. We have failed both in the practical and the spiritual fields. According to J. B. Kraus (Tokyo) the Japanese regard Christianity as an American and European product, that is to say, as "a religion without drive, able neither to prevent a World War and the other European wars nor to hinder the formation of a mass proletariat through its doctrine of Christian charity. It is only fanatical where Bible reading and good works, or movements against alcohol and smoking are concerned." Above all, the life of the European nations has not been fundamentally influenced by Christianity. Even the Christian character of the West has been denied. A Chinese Student declared: "I have now been in France for five years and have never met a Catholic student." Sadhu Sundar Singh was often told by Indians that Christianity had lost its influence on the nations and was a failure.[42]

These accusations are universal among the opponents of Christianity everywhere. N. Berdyaev wrote: "The main objection to Christianity is that it has not become a reality within the world, that it has failed – as is frequently said – that justice has not prevailed on earth, and that suffering continues in the world".[43] Christ, the Redeemer of the World, came nearly two thousand years ago, but evil, horrors, and torture continue. We have here, according to Berdyaev, the typical objection made by a false, Jewish messianism. The Jews were expecting the millennium and had therefore rejected the Messiah. The Son of God ought to have ... established the reign of goodness on earth and finally defeated evil, abolished all suffering, torment and darkness and brought eternal happiness.

In the face of these objections and expectations Berdyaev admitted that the history of Christianity was "a complete

---

[42] Friedrich Heiler, *Sadhu Sundar Singh*, p. 62.
[43] N. Berdyaev, *The Meaning of History*.

and utter failure". He held that the tasks set by Christian teaching had never been achieved and would never be achieved. Perfection existed only beyond the realm of history. The failure of Christianity, however, is no argument against its higher truth. Success and historical fulfilment are no criteria of truth and value. Moreover, these are failures of men, not of God. The failure of Christianity ought to be attributed to the fact that it was given up precisely by those who argued against it. Moreover, failure in this world does not mean final failure. The failure of Christianity is only the failure inherent in any relative world, in any limited temporal reality.[44]

It might be added, that we are not perfect and that in our inadequacy we shall never reach perfection; but we strive after it and unlike many others will never discard it. Moreover, the Scriptures nowhere refer to any full success of Christ's Church on this earth. The Bible attests very clearly that the prince of this world will have power until the end. Not even Christians themselves are promised the triumph of truth and goodness. In Christianity and in the Church there will always be tares beside the wheat, and Satan will always be at work and give scandal. We must also remember that the Church is the ark of salvation, not

[44] N. Berdyaev, ibid. 227 et seq.

a communion of perfect men; in fact, she is not the ultimate Kingdom of God; she exists not only for heroes, saints and extraordinary people, but for the sinner and the ordinary man. S. Behn said on one occasion that all the servants of the Church confess of their own accord that they are fallible sinners, "saints and shepherds not excepted". "The Church is not supernaturally great in spite of the sinfulness and fallibility of her members, but because of it. Please do understand me. What help could I obtain from a Church which consists solely of angels? I should have to stay outside. But if she is made up of men, why are we surprised at their weakness?" The same argument applies to Christianity in general.

Individually as well as collectively we have failed over and over again. We have every reason to say *nostra maxima culpa*. All the same, much that is great and wonderful has been achieved in every sphere. There are successes as well as failures, victories as well as defeats, saints as well as sinners. We find heroic virtue side by side with human weakness, heavenly inspiration side by side with earth-bound mediocrity. We have paid our tribute to the things of this world, but we have also overcome them. Peter denied Christ, but he also confessed him by his love, his teaching and his martyrdom. The same thing can be said of innumerable European Christians.

5*

Even in Asia such accusations have not been left uncontradicted. Sundar Singh wrote: "It is not Christianity that has gone bankrupt but those nations who did not understand the essence of Christianity." Paul Hsiao declared: "Individual Christians may have made mistakes, but not Christianity as such. Among men there are many robbers. But we must not hang all men because of it."

One of the most bitter accusations levelled against European Christianity is concerned with its possible dangerous after-effects. During the age of discoveries the Japanese avoided and even persecuted Catholic missionaries, since they feared they would have to share the fate of the Filipinos, Peruvians and Mexicans. A Spanish helmsman had told them that by their conversions the missionaries had paved the way for Spanish arms, and the King of Spain had conquered the world with the help of the missionaries.[45] The alliance of Christianity with the nations of Europe aroused general and long-lived suspicions. Until a few decades ago Christianity was regarded as "the slave of Western imperialism" and the ally of Western capitalism. In the meantime people have learned to discriminate, and the distinction between Christianity and the European nations has become known.[46] But even

[45] J. Schmidlin, *Katholische Missionsgeschichte*. Steyl, p. 283.
[46] Dr. Hsiao said in an address in 1946: "The German missionaries

50

now Christianity is suspect, just as in ancient times Christians were reproached for lack of civic loyalty, and their religion was thought to lead to barbarism and the disintegration of the State.

In an article entitled "Out with Christianity!" in the periodical *Daidokumin,* published before the last war by Yamakawa Seigetsu with the collaboration of high-ranking Japanese officers and several professors, we read: "Among the religions of the world there is . . . none more ruinous for our *kokutai,* our national heritage, than Christianity. The propagation of this religion would mean the sure downfall of our people. Christianity with its God and its Bible excludes every other religion, it destroys the great law that binds the subjects to their sovereign; it disobeys the Imperial Edict on Education, it disseminates dangerous ideas . . . a West-Asiatic superstition . . . it undermines . . . the progress of civilization." In September 1940 a League against Christian Organizations was founded in Japan which at its inception published the following manifesto: "Japan has had its Emperor in unbroken succession on the throne of his ancestors; it is a country of the gods, with a family system

in China have proved that Germany and German missionaries are two distinct things. Hence the missionaries could not be regarded as forerunners of Imperialism."

based upon loyalty, filial affection and faith, the legacy of the imperial ancestors. Christianity offers an illusory heaven under the fine names of liberty, equality and humanity; it forces men to believe in Jesus Christ, a sure sign of its Jewish-cunning urge for world conquest. This would radically destroy Japan's policy.... Christianity, as a Jewish plot threatening to overwhelm the spirit of the Japanese race, ought to be exterminated in Japan."

It is by reason of its novelty and its unique character that Christianity is regarded as a danger. Christianity is a foreign body, and brings about ferment and disquiet among the peoples of Asia. It disintegrates and destroys the convictions, traditions and customs fundamental to the Asian peoples. Everywhere Christianity has broken up homogeneous national communities. Again and again it has led to crises and revolutions in the countries which it entered. It has actually ruined whole nations. Tibet, Bhutan and Nepal were perfectly right in barring their frontiers to the Europeans.

These accusations contain a grain of truth. According to the words of Jesus, the kingdom of God is a leaven which penetrates and transforms everything. Christianity means crisis and judgement. Wherever Christianity gains a foothold, the world is stirred in its depths. In ancient times Christianity led to far-reaching changes, and these changes were not brought about without a struggle.[47] In the East many missionaries were and still are alienated further from the peoples than were the evangelists of the first centuries. All tensions and crises are therefore more marked. Progress and improvement on earth, however, are impossible without a struggle. Moreover, it is not Christianity and Christians that are responsible for the many unpleasant phenomena connected with the profound changes in the East to-day, but the un-Christian conduct of the representatives of the West. Nowhere in the world has so much nonsense in philosophy been produced as in Europe. Nowhere has secularism raged to such a degree as in the West. It is above all through its philosophy and secularism that Europe has become a source of unrest for Asia. The East, it is true, might have been spared much if Christianity had been united.

The dangers with which Christianity threatens the East, we are told, are especially great because of the divisions among Christian churches and sects. National communities are disturbed or even completely destroyed through these

[47] As early as the second and third centuries, pagans accused Christians of being responsible for the upheavals of the times. They were wrong. Yet Cyprian's reply, that bad times were not caused by the heathen abandoning their gods but by his opponents not adopting the true God of Christ, was equally wrong. For the empire was converted, yet perished all the same.

divisions. Europe has been broken up into nations and national Churches: even individual nations such as Germany are divided among themselves between Catholics and Protestants. In view of this development, the East should beware of Christianity. This is one of the reasons which at the beginning of the new era prevented Japan's conversion to Christianity. Father Heuvers, one time head of the Jesuit University in Tokyo, wrote: "If the Japanese – at the time when they opened their gates to foreigners and sent progressive-minded men to study conditions in Europe and America – had found a united Christendom, the country would now be Christian. But what they found was the *Kulturkampf* in Germany and hostility to and fear of religion everywhere. On returning home, therefore, they advised the authorities to ignore religion completely." In India the saying is: "Christians will bring you nothing but discord. You can see at a glance how they disagree among themselves."

Dangers threaten even where there is only one denomination involved. The individual denominations are not at all as homogeneous as they might appear. Not even the Catholic Church! It is true, we may find a formal unity in her, but among Catholics there are also far-reaching hidden divergences which are difficult to remove. In the conflict about the rites the missionaries were in opposite camps not only in trivial, but also in important matters. On one side they were in favour of the rites, on the other against them. At the time the Emperor Kang-Hsi negotiated for a long while but in the end broke off the discussions, "disgusted with the intrigues of the Christians and their bid for power" (J. Peters). He expressed himself with much asperity on the controversies between Catholics.[48] That was the end of his sympathies for the Christian faith, and any Christian missionary work was made well-nigh impossible. In other cases, too, Asians have met differences among Catholics and Catholic missionaries.

For many the Christian scale of values is a cause of fear. The Asians, for whom political values rank supreme, find it impossible to embrace a faith which will assign the highest place to God and overturns their own secular values. These Asians are in a minority but their numbers are increasing.

Another point is the universal character of Christianity. Everywhere in the East, where national elements take precedence before universal, Christianity is regarded as

[48] See Pang Ching-jen, "Documents chinois sur l'histoire des missions catholiques au XVIIe siècle" in *NZM*, vol. i (1945), pp. 39–43. After having listened carefully to both friends and opponents of the rites, the emperor came to the conclusion "that the Christian faith is no better than idolatry and the lower religions of the Buddhists and Taoists" (p. 43).

dangerous. The idea of humanity must not be emphasized more than that of the State. This criticism is levelled especially against Catholicism. An apostolic delegate told me sadly during a visit to his residence in the East: "Formerly universalism was looked upon as a point in favour the Church, now it is regarded as a danger." To-day universal religions are dropped in favour of national religions, the offspring of the old tribal religions. Some Asians are repelled by the idea of the central control of Catholicism. It is dangerous to be bound in obedience to a man who lives outside Asia beyond the sea.

The attitude of the Church on the question of the individual and the community is also a popular subject of criticism. In Japan, according to Father J. B. Kraus, S.J., Christianity is "regarded as dangerous by reason of its allegedly exaggerated encouragement of personality, democracy, liberty and equality".

Moreover, the independence of the Church from the State is looked upon as a danger. Christians form an independent community and resist any kind of submission to the State. Consequently there arose so many disputes between State and Church in Europe and America, for example, in Mexico and Germany.

Christianity is also considered to be dangerous simply because it is a faith, a religion: or in the words of Jiddu

Krishnamurti, "Beliefs, ideas divide; they never bring people together. You may bring a few people together in a group, but that group is opposed to another group. Ideas and beliefs are never unifying; on the contrary, they are separative, disintegrating and destructive. Therefore your belief in God is really spreading misery in the world; though it may have brought you momentary consolation, in actuality it has brought you misery and destruction in the form of wars, famines, class-divisions and the ruthless action of individuals."[49]

According to others, however, Christianity is a blessing for the peoples of Asia. Chiang Kai-shek, Lo Pa Hong, Coelestin Lou, Tanaka and many others regard Christianity as the salvation of Asia. A Japanese Buddhist minister said: "Japan's salvation lies in Christianity . . . Shintoism and Buddhism are dead religions."

[49] Krishnamurti, *The First and Last Freedom* (London, 1954), p. 206 et seq.

CHAPTER TWO

CHURCHES AND CHURCH ORGANIZATION

The Churches

OPINIONS are divided in Asia on the Western multiplicity of churches and denominations. Christians in Asia frequently and emphatically complain of the divisions of Christianity; some even revolt against it. Many Asian Protestants declare that they consider all differences in doctrine, cult and organization as of purely historical interest. They do not wish to be concerned with them. Disillusioned men like Sadhu Sundar Singh and Toyohiko Kagawa choose to remain outside any organized religion. The former wrote: "Sects are strange and superfluous things. There is only one God – why, then, are there so many churches? . . . If all sects were to unite in a single body, the world would come to an end, and there would be only heaven."[1] At the Lausanne Conference of the World Council of Churches (1927) it was stated: "Converts in the missions are already in full rebellion against the divisions in the Western Church and strike out boldly for unity and their own rites." Bhai Manilal C. Parekh writes, " . . . disunion among the Christians is a

[1] Friedrich Heiler, *Sadhu Sundar Singh,* p. 194.

58

standing scandal to the religion of Jesus. This along with the secularization of that faith has been a great stumbling-block to non-Christians".[2]

Moreover, the individual forms of the different churches arouse adverse criticism. There is not a single church or denomination in which one or another detail is not incomprehensible or offensive to Asian eyes or at least appears as an imperfection, not a single church which is not radically rejected by some. Not one, they argue, is ideal, not one a perfect expression of the message of Christ: all are adulterations of the true Church of Christ. Sundar Singh knows of no empirical or historical church which would continue the revelation of the primitive church. In his eyes the confessional churches are only "a relic of the caste system at the centre of Christianity".[3]

On the other hand, some Asians take a positive attitude to the Church or to one particular church and will even admire and praise her. Shi Lung extolled the Catholic Church in enthusiastic terms: this Church brought forth

[2] Bhai Manilal C. Parekh, *A Hindu's Portrait of Jesus Christ,* p. 436.

[3] Friedrich Heiler, op. cit., p. 193. Sundar Singh wished to be regarded solely as a Christian, not as a member of any particular church. He said: "The Church and Christianity are not identical" (p. 189). He was, however, "no isolated individualist", but took a positive view of the Church which for him is not a visible institution but the community of all souls belonging to Christ (p. 187).

59

the "magnificent medieval man", the "sole genuine and harmonious European". She has stood firm in face of all hostility. Through the uproar of modern dissolution her voice still rings out as the only noble human voice in our age, "reverberating like the sonorous pealing of bells above the noise and wickedness of a large city". She sits in judgement on world history, she is the conscience of the world and the guardian of morality. "Hers is the faith which combines splendour and renunciation, creates a harmony between opposites, balances freedom in devotion and discipline in dogma. She is the Church of the *philosophia perennis*, of strict rites and ceremonies, and then again of broad-minded understanding, of works of charity, of full artistic expression and depth of feeling. She need not be anxious about her continued existence." Many like him understand and appreciate the Catholic Church.

It is significant that Asians seem to discover traces of Europeanism even in some essential features of the churches. Down to their very depths all churches are supposed to be typically European or American products. A Chinese remarked, "It is not as though we thought we did not need the Church; but we ask ourselves whether its organization such as we know it, is necessary for us".[4]

[4] *Das Wunder der Kirche unter den Völkern der Erde* (Stuttgart, 1931), p. 138.

In Asia the Catholic Church is often described as "the Church of the Law". Catholics are said to have far too many laws and commandments. At the beginning of the modern missionary era the Jesuits went to much trouble to instil obedience to certain Church laws into their Chinese disciples. Sometimes they did not even risk to exact from Chinese Christians the promise to go to Mass at Easter and Christmas, to confession at Easter, to keep the fast on Good Friday and to abstain from menial work on Sundays. Even now these difficulties have not been completely overcome. Ecclesiastical law, I was told in the East, will have to be simplified. It is barely possible to teach Chinese that they commit a sin by working on Sunday or eating meat on Friday. In Korea I was told that there the Protestant denominations have more followers than the Catholic Church because – among other reasons – the latter has too many rules.

On account of the large number of laws and commandments in the Church, it is said the law of charity must suffer. There are frequent complaints about lack of charity. For example, in Kuala Lumpur an important Indian merchant complained that in spite of his social position and his membership of the Church he found it impossible to enter white society. Similar complaints are often voiced. The convert to Islam finds himself at once on a par with other Moslems. Christians, however, rarely regard and treat the Asian Christians as their brothers in Christ.

We can now understand Kagawa's efforts to create a "movement of charity", basing his "brotherhood in Jesus" above all on the precept "to love the Church not as she is, not the Church of the *status quo,* but the Church of the Cross, the Church of Love".

Nobody will be surprised if the sins of the Church or the Churches are pointed out and made much of. We quote one example from many. "If Peter could be inspired by God at one moment and by Satan the very next, how much more could others, even though they be bishops and archbishops, cardinals and popes, be not only inspired but guided by Satan for long spells of time? This has been amply proved by history. We might discount much from the severe judgements passed by Protestant authors of high repute, but there is no gainsaying the fact that the Roman Church has not been free from great blemishes and even crimes and sins. Dante, the greatest of Christian poets and a Catholic of the most devout kind, has lashed this Church with scathing criticism."[5] In answer to this, we only remark that it would be a strange thing if the human members of the Church did not occassionally show human

[5] See M. C. Parekh, *A Hindu's Portrait of Jesus Christ,* p. 415.

weaknesses. The sins of men are no argument against man as such. The sins of married people cannot be brought forward as evidence against the institution of holy matrimony, nor can an attack on the Church be based on the sins of individual Christians, especially since the Church has brought forth so many saints and continues to do so.

We shall not say much about the exterior form and structure of church buildings. Here, Asians say, is another example of Europaism. As far as their architecture, painting, sculpture, vestments, music, etc. are concerned, all churches appear European. Japanese, Chinese, and Indian styles are not chosen. In this respect, Buddhism, Islam and other Eastern creeds are more universal and sympathetic, for they adopt the traditions of their environment everywhere. Many Christians, however, prefer what is alien and European; they want paintings, statues, music and ornaments in the European style.

We meet with considerable criticism concerning the actual organization of the Church, especially her division into clergy and laity, teachers and pupils, rulers and ruled. Catholics and many other Christians believe that authority is necessary in matters of faith. They stand for a central authority in matters of doctrine, ritual and discipline. They want to see trained and consecrated priests administer the sacraments. Yet many Asians, primarily the non-Chris-

63

tians who have neither priests nor clergy and also some Protestants, are unable to accept this. They would argue with Kagawa that, if the faith be left to professionals, decay will inevitably set in. Christ, he said, was only a carpenter, not a doctor of divinity in the theological faculty of Jerusalem.

The Catholic Church would meet with a better response from many Asians if genuine spiritual leaders were more numerous and played a more prominent role than office-holders. Asians would find the Church more acceptable if the function of those in authority were more of an administrative, preserving and protective nature, while the spiritual leaders determined and fostered the spirit of the whole. Without any official status Gandhi had the most powerful influence in India, not only in political but also in religious affairs. Others occupy a similar position. The chosen people of the Old Testament had a charismatic leadership apart from their ecclesiastical officialdom; in the early Church the apostles were joined by the prophets (Acts 11:27; 13:1; 15:32; 1 Cor. 14:22 et seq.); the Church was built not only on the foundations laid by the apostles, but also on those of the prophets (Eph. 2:20). In Orthodox Christianity there are still the Starets. But to-day Catholics have few or none like them, a lack that makes itself felt especially in the East. S. Ambrose, an Indian Protestant from Royapettah, wrote: "To-day

Indians have no desire for bishops, popes and leaders of the modern managerial type, but for apostles and prophets such as the peasants and workers in the Lord's vineyard among the early Christians." The demand is for prophets who give testimony inspired by their contact with the living truth. Here the fact is overlooked that bishops and priests are both holders of office and bearers of the spirit, and that in the Church men and women without official standing have always had a far-reaching influence, as for instance St. Francis of Assisi, St. Teresa of Lisieux and many others. There is a need for many more Christians like them in Asia.

Asians have often found the authority of the bishops and priests just as irksome as the way in which it is exercised. Catholics like Yamamoto and Lo Pa Hong felt they were kept unnecessarily under the tutelage of the clergy. Lo Pa Hong told my friend P. Konrad Rapp – who was later murdered – "Clericalism is the enemy". Errors of individual bishops and priests do not, however, affect the mission of the clergy as such. Above all, their mistakes should not make us forget the services which bishops and priests have rendered and are still rendering to men and nations, nor what Pius XI and Pius XII said about the rights of the laity.

Many Asians are repelled by certain honours conferred on Christian dignitaries. Korean Christians told me they

6*

did not like Pontifical Mass since everything centred on the prelate. In reply to such criticisms we might quote the American writer, Elton Trueblood: "The Church has sometimes imitated the world in the honours she has heaped upon her dignitaries. But it remains a fact that the gospels continue to be the major weapon against the cult of power which is the worst scourge of this miserable century of ours. If they had done nothing else but to keep alive in the world the idea that humble service is better than inflated power, wise men would certainly support and foster the Church with all the means at their disposal." Bhai Manilal C. Parekh wrote that Jesus may have been the first among the great teachers to whom it was granted "to realize that love of honours accompanies religious life, and that this makes it null and void". Ambition "poisons the springs of life at their very source", and makes pious people hypocritical. It "is enough to vitiate true religious life". "It destroys the essence of religions."[6]

In Asia, as well as in the West, the esteem for the organization of the Church and consequently for the Church herself depends primarily on the conduct of the clergy. Certainly the Catholic clergy has its faults and short-

[6] *A Hindu's Portrait of Jesus Christ*, pp. 291–4.

comings. There are some egoists and climbers among them. But good and pious priests by far exceed the others, and these good priests are worthy of our admiration.

Church Organization

The views Asians hold of the organization of the churches are as varied as those of the churches themselves. On the one hand, organized religion as such, that is, the incarnation and crystallization of the inner life of faith, hope and charity, of prayer and grace, is appreciated. The Catholic Church owes her attraction not least to her clearly defined dogma, her liturgical language, commandments, precepts, and organization. On the other hand, however, the organization of the Church, "churchism", is criticized and rejected. I was told of pagans who feared all commitments inherent in actual membership of the Church, and of Christians who for years followed all the rules and then all of a sudden recoiled from their former practices. They were weary, they explained, and wanted a rest.

He who knows Asians and their religions will understand this attitude. The great religions of the East, Buddhism, Hinduism, Confucianism and Islam, are not properly organized churches with a central authority in the western sense of the word. The pre- and non-Christian world does not know of any churches as supranational communities independent of the State. Everywhere in the non-Christian world, except where it is already under the influence of Christianity, State and religion are one. Moreover, many Asians are imbued with notions of freedom, self-sufficiency and self-redemption. In every kind of church they see only a station on the road to religious stagnation and an obstacle to the free breath of religion and the piety of the heart. What is loved is boundless freedom and the solitary experience of one's own strength. The individual is the "cell of the spiritual life". If a church is necessary, then only a free and friendly community, not an organization with strict rules and a central control.

Even Christians sometimes fail to understand our Western church organization. In many countries people ask whether a church is really necessary, whether we really need "the Church", or whether it is not sufficient to lead a Christian life alone or in small groups. To-day we are faced with a No-Church-Movement, with Christians who only want to join in their worship of God, not in any other way. From China as well as from India voices are often heard that reject the whole conception of organized ecclesiastical life as being wholly foreign to the Chinese or Indian mind and therefore inimical to true indigenization. The aim is "the minimum of organization and dogma, and the maximum of the spirit of religion".

In India there is supposed to be a widespread and well-organized secret Christian movement about the members of which a Protestant missionary made the following remark: "They do not like the Western types of church organization and believe that the needs of the Eastern Church would be satisfied by far simpler forms of organized life."[7] Sadhu Sundar Singh wrote: "I respect order and principles, but not too much organization. I do not believe in the kind of organization you are building up in the West." "Faith in the Church and faith in Christianity are not identical."[8] The Church means too much, especially to Catholics. "It is a thousand pities that many Roman Catholics are less concerned with Christ than with the Church of which he is the head. They cling to the shell but neglect the kernel; they defend the Church but not her Head."[9] In Japan the Uchimura Circle published a periodical with the title *Without a Church* and adapted the doctrine of the Church to a new motto: *Extra ecclesiam salus*. Among the Protestants of Nias a "community movement" (*Sekola wa awöse*) was started, which declared: "The Church of the missionaries is the Church of the Law. Men who are firmly rooted in the gospel need no Church

[7] Friedrich Heiler, *Sadhu Sundar Singh*, p. 291.
[8] Ibid., p. 242.
[9] Ibid., p. 243.

discipline . . . Christians are not subject to Church discipline, but only to that of the Holy Ghost."

Time and effort are needed to make Asians understand what the Church means to Christians in the West; they will need time to realize that lasting effects derive only from organized religion. We Christians know only too well that the Church is subject to abuses, and ecclesiastical life has often enough suffered from them. However, we believe that the Church is necessary and useful, and its discipline essential and salutary. In any case Christ founded the Church and considered membership in it a duty. *Extra ecclesiam nulla salus.* Moreover, without the Church the majority of men would quickly become brutalized and a prey to chaos.

At the end of the last war, Dr. E. Trueblood, Professor of the Philosophy of Religion at Stanford University, wrote: "In theory it is possible to be a good man without belonging to a religious community. But the difficulties are enormous. We need to share in something that is greater than ourselves. Those who proudly claim to have their own religion and therefore to be in no need of any church fall into an angelic deception. If we were angels, we might not need any artificial aids; but as men we normally need them." "The world is bad enough *with* the leaven. It is frightening to think what it would be like *without* it."

CHAPTER THREE

CHRISTIAN TEACHING

MANY Asians receive the Christian teaching and message in a friendly spirit. When long before the arrival of the first missionaries the first Catechism found its way into Korea, which at the time was cut off completely from the outside world, its profound and simple, yet easily digestible answers to the ultimate questions made such a deep impression on Korean scholars that they accepted its teaching at once and endeavoured to follow its precepts. Christian teaching has often encountered a similar response; even many non-Christians are convinced of its truths. The fact that some continue in their external allegiance to paganism allows no conclusions regarding their convictions. Many reject conversion only for some external reason.

It is true that, in proportion to the vast population of Asia, the number of those who accept Christianity unconditionally is insignificantly small; but it is not the numbers that count.

The German writer Friedrich Heiler has told of the triumphal march of Christianity "despite all statistics" in the land of the Vedas, and of the tremendous progress of the Christian idea in India within the last hundred years. Much the same can be said of other countries. Even men like Aurobindo show traces of Christian influence. Various originally Christian ideas are used by non-Christians as a matter of course, and some genuinely Christian views are universally shared. Christian monotheism has been widely victorious and idolatry defeated nearly everywhere. In particular, Christian moral and social attitudes and principles meet with appreciation. The Christianization of the non-Christian world is indeed taking place here and now. Monogamy and the greater respect for the personality and for women are the evidence. Kagawa said: "The more deeply we penetrate into the mystery of the Cross, the more clearly we find in it the only solution to all social and moral questions as well as to our own personal problems."

Criticism of Christian Teaching

Many Asians disagree with the importance we attach to thought, research and doctrine. They find the keenness of our inquiring minds incomprehensible. In Asia it is held that European civilization overestimates thought, knowledge and intellectual training. We recognize, they will say, education and perfection mainly in the field of knowledge, and do not pay sufficient attention to ethical and religious action. Tai-Hsü said: "The East has a civilization which tends to develop the emotions; the Western way of life tends to develop reason."[1] With us religion is first and foremost a concern of the brain, not, as it ought to be, of worship and action. With European Christians thought and doctrine assume an undue importance.

But these accusations are shortsighted. In Catholicism thought and doctrine, cult and action are merged. Moreover this reproach arises from a false evaluation of the intellect and of doctrine. Catholics reject every kind of intellectualism, the absolute rule of reason, the one-sided training and application of rational powers, together with every over-emphasis attached to doctrine. On the other hand Catholics are incapable of sharing this dislike of reason and dogma. It is precisely the religions of the East with their neglect of reason, knowledge, and dogma in favour of worship and action, which demonstrate that a complete religion is impossible without due care for thought and for doctrine.

[1] Tai-Hsü, *Lectures on Buddhism* (Paris, 1928), p. 5.

Too much of it

Many Asians object to the mere quantity of our doctrine. The dogmas, they say, are too numerous and the creeds too long. The reaction of some Indian Bhils was: "This doctrine is certainly true, but difficult. We do not understand it." Others said: "There is too much to learn by heart; that we cannot do." The discontent caused by the comprehensiveness of our doctrine is so widespread and so strong that some would like to see the teaching matter reduced and more consideration to be given to the emotions. Perhaps now and then they go too far in their attempts. The world is ruled by ideas and doctrines. Truth makes free. Can it be seriously denied, however, that both preaching and teaching have suffered from an accumulation of subject matter?

Too definite

The definite and precise character of Catholic teaching is a source of irritation for many Asians. Much has been written about the pagan's and neo-pagan's vagueness of spirit. This really exists and is one of the causes of the modern world's resistance to Christianity. Nietzsche rightly declared: The real reason why men hate the truth is because it is precise." One does not like being cornered; one prefers to avoid decisions and loves evasion.

In matters spiritual one likes to be poetical, that can also be said of Asian non-Christians. As a rule most of them regard and describe even important matters only vaguely. Hence we find it difficult clearly to understand conceptions like Nirvana, Fana, Tien and Tao. A desire to wrap everything in mystery, to blur sharp outlines is uncommonly widespread. The East, according to Suzuki, is given to intuition and is therefore of necessity vague and indistinct. Above all Asians prefer to see the divine in a naturalistic-theopanistic-monotheistic twilight.[2] Both Rabindranath Tagore and his father hesitated between monotheism and theopanism. Discussions with Koreans, Japanese and others have repeatedly shown me the lack of clarity existing in many religious questions.

It is not then surprising that the precision of Catholic concepts and the definite and clear character of our doctrines meet with disapproval. A Catholic Japanese wrote that "in the East – and that includes Japan – ideas are not so precise. Consequently we find it almost embarrassing to have to express things well known to us in terms of Western concepts". They imply a loss in breadth, depth and freedom, nor are they applicable to matters alien to us. A European writer was told by a Japanese: "What

[2] By Theopanism we mean the belief that God is all, to be distinguished from "pantheism" which implies that all is God.

75

you intend to write is not exactly wrong, but it is much too rational, much too limpid, much too intellectual, in one word – much too European." In Asia, ideas and similarly words often have an uncertain, vague and fluctuating meaning which allows Asians to form associations of the mind of vast multiplicity and variety. This is not the case with our religious ideas and terms. They are sober, definite, "soulless" and do not allow for spiritual digression. This, however, is precisely what many Asians like.

The onesidedness of our religious beliefs, for example, concerning God, is also regarded as a shortcoming. It is a widespread Asian opinion that all men see only one side of the absolute. Each view is necessarily limited. A moderately satisfactory picture of the absolute can be arrived at only by combining the partial views. Christians, too, in particular Western Christians, only see certain facets of the absolute; they perceive in God, we are told, only the masculine side. Ramakrishna thought it necessary to remind Western Christians: "Do not forget the Great Mother!" Another example: Western Christians think of God always as representing merely Love, not – like the *Gita* and other Eastern writings – as being the Awe-inspiring and Sinister One, which are his indispensable characteristics. "An Indian will be surprised by the onesidedness with which the West has transfigured the divine image, emphasizing only what is mild, serene, and tranquil, whereas in actual life all parts are always next to one another and opposites dwell side by side."[3] A Catholic Japanese wrote to me: "Divine justice must be held in the same respect as divine love." A third example: God, it is said, is regarded by Christians merely as a transcendent being, not as immanent and at work everywhere in the world; in any case, Christians are much less aware of this truth. Rabindranath Tagore wrote, "I have kissed this world with my eyes and my limbs. I have wrapped it within my heart in numberless folds; I have flooded its days and nights with thoughts till the world and my life have grown one, and I love my life because I love the light of the sky so enwoven with me."[4] "In India the greater part of literature is religious, because 'God with us' is not a distant God; he belongs to our home, as well as to our temples. We feel his nearness to us in all the human relationships of love and affection, and in our festivities he is the chief guest whom we honour. In seasons of flowers and fruits, in the coming of the rain, in the fulness of the autumn, we see the hem of his mantle and hear his footsteps. We worship him in all the true objects of our worship and love him wherever our love is true.

[3] H. Zimmer, *Maya* (Stuttgart-Berlin, 1936), p. 110.
[4] R. Tagore, *Creative Unity*, p. 8.

In the woman who is good we feel him, in the man who is true we know him, in our children he is born again and again, the Eternal Child."[5]

This criticism has some justification. St. Paul writes, "We know in part, and we prophesy in part" (1 Cor. 13:9). We see and know much of God, but not all. "For who hath known the mind of the Lord?" (Rom. 11:34.) Narrowness is a peculiarity of our souls' onesidedness, a peculiarity of our vision, thinking and knowing. Psychology has shown that man is capable of paying attention to only one part of reality at a time, and of grasping only one section of it with accuracy. Others necessarily remain obscure, but onesidedness and partial vision do not inevitably imply error. We see only one side of the moon, but that does not make ours a false view. Individuals, societies, and even entire ages recognize only one or the other truth about God, but their image of him need therefore not be erroneous. Asians sometimes ask us to hold incompatible views of God.

Nor is the supernatural aspect of Catholic doctrine to the Asians' liking. Buddhists proclaim that their teaching is a doctrine of pure reason; in that respect it surpasses

[5] R. Tagore, *Personality,* p. 27 et seq. For a criticism of this attitude see S. Estborn, *The Religion of Tagore in the Light of the Gospel* (Madras, 1949), p. 76.

that of Christianity and will, therefore, be some day the doctrine of the future and of the world. The adherents of the prophet of Mecca make similar claims.

"Dogmatism", the exactness with which the divine mysteries are expressed, is severely criticized. Moslems will be able to understand this, for in their view the real truth has already been discovered; it only needs to be firmly established, formulated and its deeper meaning disclosed. Most other non-Christians of Asia have different ideas. Mao Tse-tung remarked in 1948, "Dogmas can never fertilize a field or feed a dog. Chinese intellectuals will have to forego dogmas, and construct their own theories on the basis of the reality of Chinese history and revolution from the point of view and with the method of Marxism-Leninism."[6] Devout Asians accuse Catholics of being too dogmatic. One of the sayings of the "Mother" of Aurobindo is: "The articles and dogmas of a religion are mind-made things and, if you cling to them and shut yourself up in a code of life made out for you, you do not know and cannot know the truth of the spirit that lies beyond all codes and dogmas, wide, large, and free."[7]

They say that like its buildings, so also the dogmas of the West are solid and final. In the East, on the other

---

[6] W. Chan, *Religious Trends in Modern China*, p. 263.
[7] *The Message and Mission of Indian Culture*, p. 58.

hand, no solid buildings are put up to last for ever, nor is there any desire for definite definitions and for men to be bound by them. There is no such thing as an ultimate scientific truth. "Like the surface of the ocean, thought changes perpetually", says Tai-Hsü.[8]

Radakrishnan regards it as one of the glories of Hinduism that it does not know "fixed intellectual dogmas".[9] A Hindu leader said: "There is no dogma in Hinduism. It is possible for a man to believe in any doctrine whatsoever, including atheism, without ceasing to be a Hindu. . . . We may interpret the Vedas as we feel inclined. That makes it possible to find a way out of the slavery of dogmatism."[10] Ramakrishna said: "As long as the bee is still circling round the lotos blossom, before having found its honey, it will hover round the flower making buzzing sounds, but once inside the calyx, it will drink the nectar noise-lessly. As long as men get agitated about doctrines and dogmas, they have not tasted the nectar of true faith. Once they have partaken of it, they will be silent." Most Asians are in fact undogmatic.[11] Some of their religions even

[8] Tai-Hsü, *Lectures on Buddhism,* p. 5.

[9] Tai-Hsü, ibid., p. 5.

[10] Radakrishnan, loc. cit., p. 7.

[11] D. T. Suzuki, described Zen as "free from all dogmatic . . . encumbrances".

treat their fundamental doctrines very lightly. Asians do not like being tied in any way. Large groups in China will only tolerate a Christianity free from dogma and confined to ethics. Even Christians sometimes show little understanding of dogma and do not appreciate it. In Kagawa's Bible classes for peasants, the pupils are told of the Sermon on the Mount but little or nothing of dogmas and doctrinal distinctions.

All these weaknesses are supposed to be symptoms or consequences of Europeanism or Judaism. The Catholic conception of, and teaching about God, the world and man, it is said, are essentially European – that is to say, onesided. Faith and theology are, at least to a high degree, expressions of natural dispositions and Western ways of thinking; hence many Asians have advocated that Christian religious truths should be translated into the form of Indian, Chinese, and Japanese wisdom. Yet here again, we cannot agree. The real Christian faith, in essence and content, is not European, but universal.

Can it be proved?

Rationalistic Asians reject the Catholic teaching, or at least part of it, as unproven and unprovable. Miracles are not regarded as proof. The Chinese philosopher Kang Yu-wei wrote: "I like reading the New Testament. Love of God, love of our neighbour, that is the wonderful programme of its religion. The world wants to be admonished briefly and strikingly. But what use are the miracles in the New Testament? The Holy Scriptures of the Buddhists and the Taoists are also abounding in them." In Paltoku, Manchuria, I was told by Kim, a Korean, that when he spoke to pagans of heaven and hell, they would ask: "Have you ever been there?" "Pagans", he added, "will believe only what they see."

But they go still further. Many teachings of the Church, they will say, are ostensibly false and contrary to reason. They will speak disdainfully of legends, myths, absurdities, medieval dogmas, unscientific doctrines. Here we see both European science dominating, and the spirit of Asia.

In the first instance objections are raised to our conception of God. To the Hinayana-Buddhist belief in God is foolish and unacceptable. There is no God, and in view of the evil in the world, there can be no God. It is well known that for the Buddhist human suffering is to be explained by man's own responsibility. A Chinese told me that when in China a man loses his first-born son, people say: "That is his previous life", meaning that the son died for having sinned in an earlier existence. The idea that suffering might somehow be traced back to God is carefully avoided. Before I left Bangkok, I was told by the parish priest of the pro-Cathedral about the Buddhist objections to the Catholic faith. He could not make them change their opinions though he had wrestled with these difficulties without overcoming them all his life. The Mahayana has other ideas about God than the Hinayana, but both reject the Catholic conception of God. Tai-Hsü states: "God is really a superstition."[12] Recalling a terrible air raid during the last war, a Japanese said that it was impossible for "a loving, all-knowing and almighty God" to have created this world with its abundance of horrors. The assumption that God makes man suffer "for educational purposes" is also unacceptable. Buddhism alone, they hold, is capable of explaining our suffering and of reconciling us to it. For Buddhism "denies that God is the Creator of the world of phenomena", thus "freeing him of responsibility for the suffering and misery in time"; furthermore, because it conceives of "God as a being wholly permeated with a love that dislikes to see men suffer, even though it be for the salvation of their souls", and finally, "because it explains all things and events in the world without exception as the creation of our own thoughts".

Catholic teaching about evil is equally disturbing to

[12] Tai-Hsü, *Lectures in Buddhism*, p. 48.

Asians. They find it difficult to reconcile the existence and power of evil and of the devil with the goodness and omnipotence of God. According to Bhai Manilal C. Parekh[13] our doctrine of Original Sin is "wholly wrong", "wholly untrue", "a fantastic doctrine", "extremely unfair to God".

Moslems in particular take exception to the doctrine of the Trinity. They alone, they say, represent true monotheism, whereas Christians have relapsed into polytheism. In the hospital of Ndanda in Tanganyika I heard the story of an Indian patient who had had treatment for a long time and had been given religious books to read. The authorities thought he was deriving some comfort from our religion. When he was asked whether he wanted to be baptized, he begged for time. The day before his death he at last explained: "Oh, how terrible! You believe in three Gods! I can't. I believe in the One True God." Christ is acknowledged as a prophet, but not as God. "The Moslems believe that the Jews made the mistake of denying the mission of Christ, and that the Christians erred by exceeding the bounds of promise and deifying Christ."[14]

---

[13] *A Hindu's Portrait of Jesus Christ,* p. 134 et seq. See Hassan Suhrawardy, *World Religions* (London), p. 5.

[14] Hassan Suhrawardy, loc. cit., p. 4.

The teaching about certain divine attributes, such as the wrath of God, is quite incomprehensible to many Asians. I am thinking here above all of those Indians for whom God is all love, and of the Japanese who look upon anger as wickedness of the heart. Shinto gods barely know anger and punishment. Serenity radiates over them and the whole world. After listening to a Protestant sermon dealing with the wrath of God against the unbelievers, a Japanese declared: "What a peculiar idea! A God of wrath! Children – without teaching, without education and self-discipline – may get angry, but how could I imagine a god giving way to anger? Confucius and all wise men maintained their tranquillity in all conditions of life; I do not know whether all Christians have a similar conception of God." These are misunderstandings of an anthropomorphic character. The wrath of God is not like human anger and has nothing in common with emotional outbursts. Some Christians still show the after-effects of this pagan way of thinking. Although Sadhu Sundar Singh accepts the Bible, his idea of God lacks the polarity between anger and love.

The doctrine of eternal damnation is another obstacle which St. Francis Xavier had already encountered in Japan. Hem Chandra Sarkar told me in Calcutta that in his opinion all Christians are narrow-minded, since they believe that God condemns certain people to everlasting punishment, and that this our brief life decides our eternal destiny. Even Sadhu Sundar Singh – evidently under the influence of Mahayana Buddhism, which recognizes the punishment of hell only for a limited period – assumes ultimate beatitude for most of the damned.

The doctrine of Christ's passion and death naturally meets with incredulity or derision. When, in 1579, a Chinese mandarin was told of the Saviour's death on the Cross, he burst out laughing. Here we find the explanation of the fact that during the sixteenth and seventeenth centuries the Jesuit missionaries in China did not want to have images of the Crucifixion.

A distinguished Chinese painter, who recently exhibited her paintings in America and Europe, said that she preferred Buddha to Christ because the latter had died in agony, while Buddha had a serene, smiling, painless death.

The answer to these and other objections can be found in other books. Here we should like to make the general observation: that only too often have Christians held beliefs that proved to be wrong, as for example, the immobility of the earth. The Church, however, has never claimed that such errors were part of the faith. Yet for the sake of expediency and tactics we tend to hold much that cannot always be justified in the light of truth. Only dogmas are binding. These, it is true, transcend reason, yet are not contrary to it. It cannot surprise us that many of them are, nevertheless, not accepted. Throughout the ages, our faith has been "a stumbling block".

Again and again Christians are accused of error and injustice because of our attitude to the "heathen" and their creeds. Sadhu Sundar Singh complained bitterly to Bishop Söderblom of the European custom of calling Asians "heathens". His mother, he said, had prayed to God, served and loved him "with much more warmth and devotion than a great many Christians". It was therefore absurd to call her a heathen. More people in India than in the West were leading a spiritual life although they neither knew nor recognized Christ. "Men – in Europe – live only for this world." Many among them were "incapable of renouncing worldly things, for not only their hands but also their hearts are full of them." The Western worship of man himself was worse than the worship of idols in pagan countries. "The idolaters search for truth, but I notice that people here seek only pleasure and creature comforts." "The nations of the West have sought and found science and philosophy. They know how to make use of electricity and to fly through the air. The people of the East have searched for truth. Not one of the Three Wise Men who went to Palestine to see Jesus came from the West."[15]

Catholics are told that the manner in which they disparage or altogether ignore the great thinkers of Asia and their wisdom is false and unfair. They have no understanding at all of the Asian "visionaries" and their achievements. They refuse – and wrongly so – to assimilate the wisdom of Asia into Christian thought. Many Asians say that Catholics lack impartiality and fairness. The headmaster of a Japanese girls' college said that what had always repelled him in Catholicism had been the idea that he would have to reject everything he had hitherto believed completely; he had never been able to see why his idea of the Eternal Being and the sanctification of man should be wrong.

Asian Christians, too, have reason for complaints on this score. In a letter to Nicholas Tan, a Catholic merchant in Shanghai, the well-known Catholic Chinese, Vincent Ying, put it like this: "Our superiors – foreigners – regard our national literature as childish in character and 'negligible' in quantity." Upadhyaya Brahmabandhav (d. 1907) aimed at a liberation of Christian teaching from the

[15] Quoted from Friedrich Heiler, *Sadhu Sundar Singh,* p. 201.

"trammels of European theology", a synthesis of Christian faith and Indian thought, of Christian dogma and the Indian Vedanta, and he suffered deeply from the resistance of the leading Catholic circles to his aspirations.

In this context insufficient attention is being paid to the errors of Asian "visionaries" and thinkers, or their views are underestimated, though it is true that the views about pagan learning have been coloured only too frequently by Europeanism.

Some years ago a communication from the China Mission reported that "literature in China is stupid, childish, without thought and without feeling". The time is only beginning when a fair appreciation can be expected. "Justice and natural decency demand", wrote J. Bernhart, "that our judgement of religions should be in conformity with their own supreme phenomena and claims." Classical thought found adequate appreciation only after the victory of Christianity, the philosophy of Aristotle, in fact, only through St. Thomas Aquinas. Similarly the intellectual work of thinkers like Shankara may only find proper respect and understanding in the future. This also applies to pagan creeds. A Catholic appreciation of the religions of mankind has yet to come.

St. Justin Martyr and St. Clement of Alexandria believed that Greek philosophy stemmed from the Logos and had prepared the Greeks for Christ. St. Clement says: "Philosophy was for the Greeks what the Law was for the Jews – a guide to Christ."[16] St. Basil, Gregory of Nazianzus and St. Augustine expressed themselves in a similar manner. It may be possible to find analogies with certain philosophical systems of the East, but we must not go too far in this respect and exaggerate the possible preservation of the various truths. "It is impossible for truth to absorb and preserve all convictions that have been or still are in force. Truth may well be able to amalgamate their essential content. This, however, is not always as extensive as the first impact of such a conviction may lead us to believe." The teaching Church as well as every individual must beware of "that softening of the brain which gives the same to all men instead of to everyone his due".[17]

One particular criticism is that Christians have no understanding of the sacred writings of the Indians, Chinese and other nations. Are not the Upanishads equal in value to the Old Testament, or even the New Testament? Christians, too, join the critics. The distinguished philosopher Upadhyaya Brahmabandhav wanted to see the Vedas re-

[16] *Strom.* I, p. 5. See also I, p. 17 and II, p. 1.

[17] S. Behn, "Kirche und Wirklichkeit" in *Hochland*, 21/II (1924), p. 303.

cognized as an authority equal in value to the Old Testament, or even as the Old Testament of India. In India the Vedas should be treated as a preparation for Christ, side by side with the Old Testament, and as a means of explanation. In Japan there is a movement to replace the Old Testament by the Kojiki. Obviously these are unacceptable demands.

Is Christian Teaching Christian?

Occasionally the criticism is voiced that our doctrine is not even truly Christian. When asked for a correct interpretation, however, Asians will introduce alien ideas into Christ's message. A few examples will suffice. According to Rabindranath Tagore, Christ's teaching is the chief witness for the Indian doctrine that all men can become identical with the deity. "Though the West has accepted as its teacher him who boldly proclaimed his oneness with his Father, and who exhorted his followers to be perfect as God, it has never been reconciled to this idea of our unity with the infinite being. It condemns, as a piece of blasphemy, any implication of man's becoming God. This is certainly not the idea that Christ preached, nor perhaps the idea of the Christian mystics, but it seems to be the idea that has become popular in the Christian West."

91

The words "Before Abraham was, I am" were misinterpreted by Tagore.[18] Dr. Ukita, a Japanese Christian, who suggested with reference to the Bible passage about God, the prime mover, that Christianity should introduce the Buddhist doctrines of the immanence of God, revealed a similar misunderstanding of the Bible.

Sometimes Christians are said to understand inadequately, or even to misunderstand, the personality of Jesus himself. Most Asians find Christ congenial and acceptable. The impression he made was and is still tremendously strong, so strong that, for example, Neo-Islam transferred some of his features to Mohammed. But it is widely held that the image of Christ must be freed from the rigidity and erroneous conceptions of the West and that he must be regarded as an Asian. Christ was not European but Asian, the "noblest" of all Asians, and there are many who believe that Christ was an Indian. To follow Tagore's view is indeed to hold that Christ has been misunderstood by Christians throughout the ages.

The ideas which Stanley Jones expressed in his book, *The Christ of the Indian Road,* have become widely known. According to this author Christ has begun to capture the Indian people, in particular, their best minds. But what

---

[18] R. Tagore, *Sadhana,* p. 208 et seq.

attracts Indians first and foremost is Christ when detached from Western civilization, from Western creeds and
dogmas. Dogmas divide, his unique personality unites all
men. Indians should create Christian dogmas and forms
of expression best adapted to their national character.
Understanding of the spiritual life, tranquillity and devotion *(bhakti)* would then become characteristics of Indian
Christianity. This criticism, too, is significant.

Too rational and not enough Feeling

Christian teaching is based upon Revelation, that is, upon
faith. The doctrine expounds Revelation, theology
represents a knowledge of faith. Many Asians do not find
this easy to understand. There are mystics in Asia who
consider our faith a lower stage of knowledge. Man is not
in their opinion in need of historical revelation but can
arrive at truth independently through experience and by
listening to his inner voice.

Many Asians criticize the Church's teaching that Revelation was closed once and for all through Christ and his
Apostles. Most of them believe that divine life springs
eternally from new sources and they wish to be granted
immediate experience of the divine. T. Suzuki blames
the Western Christians for holding that every "original
experience . . . could only be heterodox".

Rabindranath Tagore attributed the atrophy of religion to the deification of the past. Sadhu Sundar Singh did not confine divine revelation to the historical figure of Jesus. In answer to this it is, above all, to be remembered that, as the Church teaches, only the universal and public revelation has come to an end with Christ and the Apostles, but that individual revelations have continued to occur and may occur again. Here it is relevant to quote from the *Imitation of Christ* (iii, 3, 5): "I taught the prophets from the beginning, saith the Lord, and cease not to speak to all men even until now." It is, however, unlikely that Asians will be satisfied with these sentiments.

Many Asians are repelled by the part played in Western Christianity by discursive reason in the search for truth and in the interpretation and penetration of religious facts.

In the sphere of religious truth and reality reason is supposed to have no authority. The Catholic trust in the powers of reason is said to be altogether misplaced. We indulge in an exaggerated optimism. In the realm of religious truth, Asians will say, reason only leads us astray; it leads to doubt and other pitfalls. The greatest restraint is necessary. Gandhi held: "'*Neti*' (not this) was the best explanation of Brahma (God) that the authors of the Upanishads were able to give." As early as the fourth and fifth centuries Orientals violently objected to the Greeks for introducing their logic and love of philosophy into Christianity. According to Ephrem faith is a mystery, not something to be argued about and pondered. The Syrian Pseudo-Dionysius expressed the Eastern idea that God is wholly inaccessible to our thoughts. "By the process of knowledge we can never know the infinite being, but if he is altogether beyond our reach, then he is absolutely nothing to us. The truth is that we know him not, yet know him."[19] "He (Brahma) can be known by joy, by love. For joy is knowledge in its completeness, it is knowing by our whole being. Intellect sets us apart from the things to be known, but love knows its objects by fusion. Such knowledge is immediate and admits of no doubt. It is the same as knowing ourselves, only more so."[20]

Jiddu Krishnamurti wrote, "Thought has not solved our problems and I don't think it ever will ... ideas do not solve any of our human problems; they never have, and they never will."[21]

Laotse said: "The name which is intelligible is not the name of the Eternal." Confucius: "We know nothing about life, how, then, can we know death?" The thoughts

[19] Rabindranath Tagore, *Sadhana,* p. 154.
[20] Ibid., p. 159.
[21] *The First and Last Freedom* (London, 1954), p. 111.

95

of most Confucian thinkers run on similar lines. Ku Hung Ming, known for his hostile attitude to the West, confined himself to practical ethics, evading the ultimate problems of our beginning and our end. Professor Yoshimitsu told me in Tokyo that in Japan the conception of mystery was powerful. The opinions of Japanese Buddhists are known. Suzuki regards philosophers as "builders of sandcastles" and philosophy as "much ado about nothing". "It only goes to show how at all times philosophers have contradicted each other." "Truth becomes manifest only when we have cast off all intellectual dishonesty and other absurdities and return to our primitive nakedness."

Occasionally even Christians show a lack of understanding here. Life in a theological college gave rise to Sadhu Sundar Singh's profound aversion to theological intellectualism and hair-splitting. Kagawa wrote: "We must not try to apprehend God by our reason but . . . to live as God's children." A blind man visited Juji Ishii, the Christian philanthropist. He was supposed to be uneducated and unable to read. He asked Ishii to instruct him in Christianity. Ishii told him: "You will see God if you give the money that you earn to a blind man poorer than yourself." The blind visitor obeyed and after a fortnight declared: "Master, I have grasped it: God is Love."

But intellectualism is also rife in the East, sometimes more so than in the West. In India, for instance, knowledge as such holds a pre-eminent position and is often even considered as the sole path to salvation. The urge to metaphysical speculation is innate in Indians as only in few other races.

However, we must state as a matter of principle that we consider faith and intuition, as well as reason, as ways of apprehending the truth. There is a conception of reality which is not based on logical conclusions, as for example, the artistic apprehension of being. This, too, is knowledge.

Catholics are convinced of the inscrutability of the Divine Majesty and of the frailty of the human mind. Our knowledge of divine truth is inadequate, hence its perfect understanding is impossible. Moreover, we by no means deny that all purely rational inquiries into the nature of God, the world and man may lead to difficulties that cannot be solved with our natural equipment; for example, reason will show us that God is the cause of all that exists, and that man is free, but not how these two established truths are compatible. Nevertheless, we trust reason, one of our finest gifts, and count its use among our most precious activities. Reason, when used in the right way and within due limits, will lead towards the knowledge of funda-

8*

mental truths concerning the natural order. Only the form of rationalism which expects everything from reason and makes of it an arbiter of truth must be rejected.

Reason has its rightful place even in the realm of the religious mysteries, where it is most valuable and indispensable to the Church. Catholics seek to define the data of revelation, as far as this is possible, and to make them their own. Faith is examined in order to find the connections between the different religious truths. The Church has never been content with the mysteries of the faith alone, but has always pursued the study of theology. Pure rationalism begins only when the fact is forgotten that many things transcend our powers of reasoning, when everything is rejected that cannot be rationally explained, and when, consequently, revelation is measured by reason. Catholic theology is not rationalistic but rational – in so far as it submits to the laws of logic.

Asians, however, consider even this moderate use of reason as foolish and presumptuous. "Latin rationalism" is suspect. Great theological controversies are unknown to them. There is no reverence for what is most sacred. The horizontal, not the vertical, is the mark of Eastern spirituality. People cling humbly to the earth. They "prostrate themselves before the mystery" and listen to the revelations of this world. Junyu Kitayama wrote: "Within the Christian faith God, in all his magnificence and splendour, was quite close to the Christians once they had left the finite spirit of wanting to know everything." He referred to St. Francis of Assisi and Eckhart. Christians of their kind have deeply impressed the Japanese and have met with immediate understanding. Many Asians would agree with Kitayama when he says: "It must suffice to have explored the explorable and to worship the inexplorable with tranquillity."

Chinese philosophers know of "no strict rules of logic". Tales, anecdotes, legends, stories and the like play a larger part in their dogmas than logical thought. The philosophers adapt themselves to Chinese ways of thought. This does not mean that the Chinese are incapable of logic. In the opinion of Paul Hsiao Catholics are outwardly logical, but the Chinese pursue an inner logic.[22] They are not acquainted with the logic of the West, but familiar with that primitive logic which all men possess or ought to possess. This author, at least, admits the values of Western logical systems. Others, however, go farther. According to Suzuki, logic, "the characteristic expression of Western thought, has always been the ruin of man-

[22] In his Preface to J. C. H. Wu's book, *The Interior Carmel* (London, 1954), p. ix, Archbishop Yupin of Nanking writes that "logic" appears too cold to the Chinese, who prefers a genuine act of love.

kind;" it is not only useless but positively harmful. Instead the Zen practice strives to "rise above logic" and "find a superior realm of truth which precludes all controversy".[23] The end in mind is "the abandonment of rational thought",[24] and concentration on personal experiences. It is significant that the objections to Christianity are in most cases not on the logical plane.

Similar views prevail in the churches of the Near East. Ivan Kireievski wrote in *Russia's Criticism of Europe* that the main characteristic of the Roman spirit consisted in the preponderance of external rational elements over the intuition of the essence of things. He and other Russian writers held that the spirit of ancient Rome and of the Roman Church were identical. Revealed truth is recognized by way of intuition, but the Roman Church – they believed – by her use of logical concepts and scholastic syllogisms has transformed faith into science.

We do not find these attacks convincing. The competence of logic can certainly be – and often has been – exaggerated. St. Nicholas of Cusa said: ". . . the boast of logic does the sacred knowledge of God more harm than good" and mentions with joy the ejaculatory prayer of St. Jerome: "Oh Lord, deliver us from the dialecti-

[23] Suzuki, *Die große Befreiung.*
[24] Jung, in his Introduction to *Suzuki,* ibid., p. 30.

cians." Logic renders us useful service all the time, even in the religious sphere; yet it is not the one and only means to understand and express religious truths. Other methods can and must supplement it.

Asian critics will argue that we are sadly lacking in intuition of divine truths. Religion to them is intuition, vision, experience. That, according to S. Radhakrishnan, is the "superiority of Hinduism". Hem Chandra Sarkar, the venerable blind president of the Sadharan Brahmo Samaj, told me in Calcutta: "God has given our soul power to recognize him directly. God is in our soul." And Rabindranath Tagore wrote: "We cannot attain the supreme soul by successive additions of knowledge acquired bit by bit even through all eternity, because he is one, he is not made up of parts; we can only know him as heart of our hearts and soul of our soul; we can only know him in the love and joy we feel when we give up our self and stand before him face to face." We are not quite clear about the exact meaning of the word "vision", nor is there any way of ascertaining the facts. We believe that men walk by faith and not in the fulness of sight. The beatific vision is reserved for the next world or for special moments of grace in this one. However, in this life, there is already a kind of dim vision which fore-shadows the vision of heaven. In general philosophy is hard work. The Middle Ages knew reason, *ratio,* "the power of discursive thought, of research and discrimination, of abstraction and judgement" and worked with it. But since the philosophers of antiquity, the Greeks, even Plato and Aristotle, men have known "an element of purely passive intuition or, in the words of Heraclitus, of 'listening to the essence of things'[25] in the cognitive faculty" as well as in his sense perception. Medieval philosophy knew discursive reason, but also intuition, "the faculty of *simplex intuitus,* the 'simple gaze' before which truth lies open as a landscape does beneath the eye". By virtue of this faculty man can share in the order of pure spirits.[26] These are facts and possibilities which Asians might ponder when they speak of vision and the desire to see.

The West, it is said, lacks not only intuition of divine truth, but its experience as well. We know of God and his works by inference, while Asians experience the absolute. We speak of a remote reality; Asians, of one close at hand. In Hinduism, in the words of S. Radhakrishnan, "dogma is experience" and "the inner experience dominates the external expression". For Sadhu Sundar

[25] J. Pieper, *Leisure and Culture* (Faber and Faber, 1950).
[26] Ibid., p. 26 et seq.

Singh, the opponent of all "clever syllogisms", it is "real-ization" that matters. Religion means experience of the Divine in the depths of the soul. The East prefers experienced truth to the truths of faith.[27]

Does this experience of the Divine really exist in Asia wherever it is spoken about? We doubt it. Certainly any purely rational knowledge of God can and should be supplemented by empirical knowledge. Any knowledge attains its greatest perfection when the whole man is engaged in it; the knowledge of God, when it is also based upon likeness and kinship, on union and communion. It is above all in Christianity that *cognitio experimentalis* of God can be found.[28]

Finally, we are told that there is no place in Christianity for emotion. Asians would greatly prefer an emotional religion to one dominated by faith. They are fond of quoting from Goethe's *Faust* that "Feeling is everything, a name is but an empty sound". Piety is normally connected with the emotions; they have their due importance in religion. However, the emotions are not the origin or source of religion, but arise from and

[27] Kitaro Nishida, *Die intelligible Welt,* p. 118: "Of the content of religious consciousness it can . . . only be said that it is experience."
[28] St. Thomas Aquinas deals with the *cognitio experimentalis Dei,* particularly in conjunction with the donum sapientiae.

with it; they are not essential, but accidental elements. Religion must not exhaust itself in emotions. Here, as everywhere else, all excess must be avoided.

Too many Words

The wording of Christian teaching is often criticized in truly Asian fashion. In religious practice Asians like to dispense altogether with words. When referring to God, Hinduism states: "Silence is superior to speech". The ancient visionaries spoke of the divine "obscurity", of that "of which nothing can be said". "Not through speech, not through thinking, not through vision can it (the Atman) be grasped."[29] In the Tao-te-king we read: "He who knows the Divine, needs no words; whoever needs words, does not know it." The Buddhist Dhyana-School (Chinese Ch'an, Japanese Zen) puts no confidence in words; they only obscure the truth or, in the best of cases, hint at it. Suzuki, an adherent of the Zen sect, declared: "There is no real value in words like God, Buddha, soul, the Infinite, the One."[30] The famous Japanese philosopher Kitaro Nishida has not been able to express the Ultimate, the absolute "Nothing". "It might

[29] *Kathaka-Upanishad,* vi, 12.
[30] Suzuki, loc. cit., p. 106. Zen even mocks at words like "monotheistic".

be called 'the world of mystical vision' inaccessible to word and thought alike."[31] For the Japanese, writes Kikuaki Ogata, faith cannot really be expressed in words, which are merely hollow symbols.

The great Western thinkers and theologians are well aware of the limitations and impotence of words. St. Augustine confessed: "No power of expression could ever match my knowledge."[32] And again: "We then returned to the clamour of speech, to the words that begin and end in our mouths. But what have they in common with thy Word, our Lord, the Word that exists in itself?"[33] It cannot be denied that words tend both to conceal and to reveal the mystery. All the same, the word retains its value; in general it exceeds all other ways of expression. As far as dogmatic formulae are concerned, we must distinguish between form and content. The content is eternal and absolute, its expression is temporal and inadequate without being false. Dogma, wrote the German theologian, H. Straubinger, "does not claim to offer a perfectly rational and appropriate expression of the mystery; neither is it a faltering approximation to truth, but a clearly defined formulation of facts as revealed

---

[31] K. Nishida, *Die intelligible Welt*, p. 117.
[32] *De Trin.*, xv, 45.
[33] *Conf.*, ix, 10, 23.

by God. This leaves the possibility of a future, more profound and more exact interpretation without abandoning the earlier dogma."[34]

Even the character of our language meets with criticism; our theological idiom, and in particular the wording of our dogmas, have a purely Western character. This is only natural since it is of predominantly European origin. It is quite likely that a different environment would have produced different versions. The real meaning may find its expression in Indian, Chinese or Japanese. Why, however, should the Western expression of a dogma be identical with misinterpretation?

The reasons for these linguistic objections, however, lie deeper. The languages and writings of the East are to a large extent flexible, vague and ambiguous. What we regard as a defect means superiority to Chinese, Koreans and Japanese. Asians are fond of using word pictures and parables when speaking of sublime things, as anyone knows who is familiar with the religious literature of Asia. Buddha and Yajnavalkya are the obvious examples. Asian Christians share this propensity. Kagawa avoids abstract and didactic verbiage when speaking and writing about God; he uses parables and images instead. Sadhu

---

[34] H. Straubinger, "Gnosis, Glaube und Theologie" in *Tübinger Theologische Quartalsschrift,* 123 (1942), pp. 262 et seq.

Sundar Singh scorned the logical idiom, replacing it by imagery and parables. Christ, with his images and parables is here the supreme ideal.

Asians raise objections also to the verbosity of Western theology. In dealing with the divine – as in art – thrift in the use of words is indicated. European painting, in spite of many exceptions, is far more concerned with naturalistic reproduction of details than is Asian art. The art of the Far East is less naturalistic and less concerned with reality. Sometimes there is only a slight indication. A few strokes give an intimation of the whole; a blossom, a twig, the outline of a simple landscape convey a vision of the Infinite. European art, therefore, appears to Asians superficial, incapable of penetrating into the depths. Similar remarks are made about Western languages, including their theological idioms.

Some thinkers disapprove of our teaching and theology as being too systematic. Hsiao thought that the Chinese had no system. This did not mean that everything was in confusion; there is an inner coherence. "The living, 'developed' Buddhism of Japan", according to the Buddhist Ohasama, "never proceeds systematically. It will and must be without a system."[35] Rabindranath Tagore

[35] Schuej Ohasama and A. Faust, *Zen,* xv.

wrote: "The poet's religion is fluid like the atmosphere around the earth, where light and shadow play at hide-and-seek, and the wind, like a shepherd boy, plays upon its reeds among flocks of clouds. It never undertakes to lead anybody anywhere to any solid conclusion, yet it reveals endless spheres of light, because it has no walls round itself."[36]

What can we reply to this? We also present truth in ways familiar to many Asians, as in the Bible and in the Liturgy. These are not systematic like the *Summa Theologiae* of St. Thomas Aquinas. In order to counter all attacks on systematic thought it must be pointed out that the desire of the human spirit to build individual doctrines into a system in order to survey the whole is legitimate. The entire world of reality and truth is organically bound together. It cannot be wrong to wish that this coherence, this unity of creation, should be expressed in a system. The human spirit needs breadth, order and cohesion.

As for Tagore's aesthetic religion, it may be said that such a religion helps man to evade God and his demands and is consequently very imperfect. "Beauty is not the whole truth." A river needs banks.[37]

[36] R. Tagore, *Creative Unity,* p. 16. See Nietzsche's words: "I suspect all systematicians and keep out of their way. The desire to create a system springs from a lack of intellectual integrity."

[37] S. Estborn, *The Religion of Tagore in the Light of the Gospel* (Madras, 1949), p. 175.

Instruction and Books are unpopular

Religious instruction, as such, is unpopular with many Asians. Rabindranath Tagore rejected religious instruction, because he was convinced that everyone must find his own religion and can do so only by experience.

Books which expound our doctrine also meet with adverse criticism. The aged Bodhidharma (Japanese: Daruma), the famous patriarch of Buddhism, had little regard for any books, even "Holy" writings.

There is the Ch'an School, or school of meditation, which expects insight to come from "an abrupt enlightenment by calmly looking into one's own mind to discover the Buddha-nature and instantly intuit the Void". Philosophical systems and books are considered superfluous. Everything centres round the development of a technique of concentration and intuition.[38] This religious technique is best known in the form of Zen-Buddhism.

Only by experience, it is said, does man gain access to books and pictures. Daisetz Teitaro Suzuki wrote: "Life itself has to be grasped in the fulness of its flow; it must perish if we stem it in order to examine and analyse it, and we are left with the lifeless body in our arms."[39]

---

[38] W. Chan, *Religious Trends in Modern China,* p. 94.
[39] D. T. Suzuki, *Die große Befreiung,* p. 185.

"All so-called sacred books (of the Buddhists) are but rubble."[40] Arguments of this kind are nowadays welcomed by many Christians. Kagawa, a Christian, said: "Do not seek God in books. Only in love is God revealed. He who desires to hear God's voice must love. God is recognized best where love is most perfect." Many are tired of books. Some desire direct access to truth, others a relationship as between master and pupil; that relationship which existed in antiquity, in medieval Christianity and still exists in Asia. There is nothing wrong with this desire, but we have good reason not to discard books, especially The Book.

[40] Ibid., p. 52.

CHAPTER FOUR

FORMS OF DEVOTION

THERE are some Asians who despise not only the conventional forms of devotion, but devotion itself. This applies in the first place to the adherents of modern secularism, but to others as well, among them many representatives of Mahayana Buddhism. Daisetz Teitaro Suzuki praises Zen Buddhism for having no God to worship and no religious rites to observe, in short, for being free of all "religious encumbrances". Religious pictures and services are on the whole of little value. Zen would say, "Do your devotions before the camelia as it opens its blossom and worship it, if you so desire. This is as much a religious experience as prostrating yourself before the Buddhist deities, or sprinkling holy water or receiving Holy Communion."[1]

Most Asians, on the other hand, value devotion very highly. Gandhi said: "Nobody can live without religion." "Worship of God is the supreme privilege of man", writes

[1] D. T. Suzuki, loc. cit., p. 53.

Hem Chandra Sarkar in his edition of the Brahmo Prayer Book. For Asians of the old school everything is religion, and religion is everything. A religious foundation is the mainspring of life. The masses of most Eastern countries can be guided only by religious slogans. A man without religion is no real man, but a monster. The infinite truth, love and holiness of God must in some way attract the true man, as the North Pole attracts the magnetic needle.

The late Aga Khan, head of the Ismaili sect, said that for him "that greater spiritual love and enlightenment, the fruit of that sublime experience of the direct vision of reality which is God's gift and grace, surpasses all that the finest, truest human love can offer. For that gift we must ever pray". And he continued, "I have been told that Buddhists, Brahmins, Zoroastrians, and Christians have also attained this direct, mystical vision. I am certain that many Moslems, and I am convinced that I myself, have had moments of enlightenment and knowledge of a kind which we cannot communicate because it is something given and not something acquired."[2] A Buddhist writer who discussed the problem of atomic energy concluded: "A change of mankind's mental attitude through religion

[2] *The Memoirs of the Aga Khan* (London, 1954), p. 171.

is the only solution. What is necessary at the moment is the mastery over mind and not only the mastery over matter."[3]

Small wonder, then, that Asians are astonished and disconcerted when faced with religious apathy, worldliness, and even complete religious indifference among many Europeans and Americans.

Most inhabitants of Christian countries have, in the opinion of Sadhu Sundar Singh, "a white face and a black heart. In pagan countries I saw people enter their temples; they are God-fearing. Here (in Europe) people seek nothing but pleasure. They (the pagans) strive after peace, but in Europe people are content with worldly prosperity". Sadhu Sundar Singh gravely blamed the Western nations for their de-Christianization, their religious indifference, their craving for money and pleasure. Christian nations are threatened with a severe judgement at the end of time. "You Westerners live in too much of a rush; you have time neither to pray nor to live." "Men who do not live, through their prayer, in communion with God, are not worth being called human, they are like trained animals." Our theologians find scant praise. "They spend too much time with their books and not enough with the Lord."

---

[3] Hba Sithu U Ba Khen, *What Buddhism Is* (Rangoon), p. 85.

9*

Even the piety that still exists in the West is not approved by many Asians. Its religious life, they say, is wanting in seriousness and depth. Before the Second World War members of the Gaudiya-Mission, which I had previously met in India, opened a house in London and undertook lecture tours through various European countries. They found the state of religion in Germany appalling. Only in the Benedictine Abbey of Beuron did they feel at home.[4] Sadhu Sundar Singh declared: "Western men are educated solely in science and philosophy, they have no understanding of spiritual values."[5] This lack of depth and integrity, it is alleged, is evident in Western man's incapacity for meditation. When a member of an Indian polo team, that had been playing in Germany, was asked about his impressions of Europe, he answered that what struck him most was that Europeans did not meditate.

Indeed, often enough Western Christianity seems to have more religious organization than actual piety. Often enough we lack that deep contemplation and enthusiasm for which we pray in the Preface of Christmas: *ut in invisibilium amorem rapiamur* – "that we may be drawn to the love of things unseen". In the cinema and at sports

---

[4] B. H. Bon, *My First Year in England* (London); by the same author: *Second Year of the Gaudiya Mission in Europe* (1935).

[5] Friedrich Heiler, *Sadhu Sundar Singh*, p. 233.

events people seem to forget to cough. They are completely absorbed. But at Mass?

Western piety is said to lack concern for essentials. The members of the Gaudiya-Mission observed that Christians seemed to remain on the borderline of piety. We might do well to recall that the early Christians directed their prayer to the Father, "that every tongue should confess that the Lord Jesus Christ is in the glory of God the Father" (Phil. 2:11). They approached the Father and brought their petitions to him through Christ. We still use this form of prayer, but not as much as in earlier ages. Those familiar with non-Christian religions will know that in many of them "the Father" tends to be forgotten and spirits take his place in the prayers of the faithful. The Father is only remembered in moments of dire distress when all other means have failed. Christians, too, suffer from this tendency, as our hymnals and books of prayer prove. There are only few prayers and hymns to the Father.

There are Asians who consider the manifestations of Christian piety a purely external practice. Bhai Manilal C. Parekh wrote: "Outward forms of religion such as sacrifices and ceremonies, rites and rituals, church membership and Sunday attendance in churches have taken the place of real religion."[6] Yet there are others who con-

[6] *A Hindu's Portrait of Christ,* p. 499.

115

sider Western Christians to be lacking in external forms of piety.

In India it is easy to discover which God a man serves. Hindus perform their ablutions in the sacred rivers publicly. No Shintoist is afraid of clapping his hands and praying in public before the sacred shrines, no Moslem of performing his *salat* in his workshop, in the market place, in the office, in the train, on the boat. But Westerners are never seen at their prayers; they show no religious fervour. There may be some who do not pray because they have no faith at all; some regard prayer as a waste of time; for others religion is a matter of the mind, of complete privacy. In the East, too, there have always been people without regard for expression and form in their piety. According to Djalal al-Din Rumi, the Lord said to Moses: "What are words to me? I need a warm heart; if you set hearts aflame in love, you need not heed thought or expression." In general, however, the East is different. Most people wish to express themselves and expect guidance from outside, as is shown by the *mudras* in Hinduism and Buddhism. Western expressions of devotion are said to be inadequate and to make no impression. As an example, there is the carelessness of most Christians when genuflecting or making the sign of the Cross. The Shintoist bows with great reverence before the *kamis*. I have never attended a Christian service which showed greater outward dignity than that displayed in a Zen Buddhist service in the monastery of Tsurumi near Yokohama.

The way in which Moslems perform their *salat* commands admiration and respect. "Christians . . . often seem to approach their God with less respect than they are accustomed to show in the presence of a government official. That we who profess to know God and to walk with him, whose Church treasuries are rich with mystic experience and glorious liturgy, should fail to show that we delight to know him with every known resource of art and every true sign of awe and reverence, is a tragedy; and in the neighbourhood of critical Moslems, a costly one."[7]

The attitude of many Christians to what is or is not specifically religious does not meet with understanding everywhere in Asia. Ramakrishna wrote, "First acquire the love of God (*bhakti*) and all the rest shall be added unto you. First is the love of God, action follows. Works without the love of God are useless and of no lasting value." A conversation with Caitanya monks

[7] *The Christian Life and Message in Relation to Non-Christian Systems.* Report of the Jerusalem Meeting of the International Missionary Council, 1928 (London, 1928), p. 273.

117

in Calcutta gave me much food for thought. They intimated that the "social gospel"[8] as represented especially by English and American missionaries was a misinterpretation of Christianity and of religion altogether. The first place in religion is due to the worship and love of God. Similar verdicts are frequently heard. Social work and active brotherly love, it is admitted, are good and necessary. But they are not of primary importance and have to take their place after redemption and the love of God; Asians have a much deeper insight here. Yuigahama said reproachfully: "Protestant Christianity may help us to attain happiness on earth, but does not promise everlasting life hereafter. It is the duty of true religion to give its followers such a promise." For some Asians even missionary work is of secondary importance. When a Benedictine monk in Tokwon Abbey (Korea) answered the question why did the brothers live in celibacy, by referring to their undivided devotion to mission work, a Japanese civil servant interrupted: "Oh, I thought that it made it possible to love God more deeply." Even Christians like Kagawa, who is himself a social thinker and worker, reject the purely or predominantly social gospel of a great many Anglo-Saxons.

[8] Bhai Manilal C. Parekh in *A Hindu's Portrait of Jesus Christ,* p. 491, calls the "social gospel" the "gospel of the Pseudo-Protestants".

These views of the relation between the love of God and the love of man, between devotion and *caritas,* are basically right. But this criticism applies only to certain, not to all Anglo-Saxon Christians. This is well-known in Asia. Kondo Yuigahama wrote many years ago in the *Japanese Times and Mail:* "Catholicism is above all a religion, not only an intellectual or cultural movement whose aim is of necessity 'social' and therefore, by its very nature, 'non-absolute'."

In the Catholic's attitude to God and communion with him sin plays a large part. He faces God as a sinner. Every day, during Mass and in the Office, the *Confiteor* is said, sometimes not less than four times. The more he has advanced in sanctity, the more profoundly conscious he is of sin, and the more sensitive his conscience becomes. A high-ranking Chinese official was asked what impression the Christ of the Gospels had made upon him, and replied: "He appears to have the power to make our consciences more sensitive."[9]

Not all Asians like such consciousness and confession of sins. According to Yoshida Masao, we sin only when – as in Christianity – "we regard man as a weak, sinful creature". "Here we find the fundamental error of human

[9] *The Christian Life and Message,* etc., p. 53.

faith. .... We must begin by rousing ourselves from this error in order to discover that the visible, physical man is not the essential being, but the mere shadow of our thoughts, and that the real man, as God created him, stands behind the visible body. .... The real man is not mortal, but lives forever in union with God."[10] The Indian writer, Sri Vivekananda, said: "It is the greatest lie of all to say that we are men. We are the God of the universe. We have always worshipped ourselves. The most untruthful thing ever said about us was the lie that we are sinners or wicked." The majority of Asians, however, would seem to think and feel differently. Upadhyaya Brahmabandhav declared himself absolutely opposed to this "monstrous, blasphemous thesis" of Vivekananda. "We shall not leave the battlefield before we have utterly destroyed this doctrine." Kitaro Nishida, educated as a Buddhist and still closely connected with Buddhism, wrote: "If someone says that he need not be ashamed of his conscience, he is only saying that it is insensitive. He who is deeply conscious of his guilt knows himself best. .... Only he who is most keenly aware of the depth of his wickedness, who cannot find a way to atonement, will be blessed with the vision of God's sacred light".

[10] See *EMZ* 5 (1944), p. 242.

Severe criticism is levelled against the lack of disinterestedness in our devotion. It is said that Catholics are guided by considerations of punishment and reward. For many people the idea of heaven and hell is more effective than the thought of God himself. Consequently in pastoral work Catholics are believed to make too much of threats of punishment and the promises of reward. These are held to be primary motives for our commandments and prohibitions. The German catechism used to teach: "We are on earth to know God, to love God, and to serve God, and to reach heaven by these means." The most important Asian religions, on the other hand, or at least certain branches of them, do not seek the satisfaction of the self, but its complete obliteration as the final perfection; indeed redemption is expected through the extinction of the self.[11]

Adherents of the Shinto religion blame Catholics for their self-seeking. The Japanese, Toyofumi, declared with distinct allusion to Christianity, that Shintoist prayers were not concerned with individuals and their needs, but with gratitude and service. Laotse's Tao is essentially unselfish and detached. Perfection and union with Tao can be attained only through self-effacement.

[11] See Thomas Ohm, *Die Liebe zu Gott in den nichtchristlichen Religionen* (Freiburg, 1957).

The essential element of devotion in Hinayana Buddhism is the freedom from desire which springs from the knowledge of man's inability to see things and himself as he is. The cause of all suffering lies in his "thirst", his desire to be, to own, to seize and to hold. The condition for the end of this suffering is the extermination of this "thirst". By harbouring desires man will prolong and increase his sufferings. Buddhism demands an uncompromising struggle against the self; an attack not only against the worldly, but also against the spiritual self, which only too willingly would take the place of its bigger brother.

Mahayana Buddhism, although it differs from Hinayana, also preaches self-lessness. Zen claims the "secret virtue" which implies: "Do good without any expectation of appreciation and gratitude. A child is about to drown. I jump into the water to save it. That is all. It has been done, continue on your way, don't look back, don't remember. . . . That is what Zen calls 'an act without merit' *(anabhogacarya)*. Jesus said: 'But when thou dost alms, let not thy left hand know what thy right hand doth; that thine alms be in secret . . .' (Matt. 6:3–4). That in the eyes of Buddhism is 'secret virtue'. But when the Gospel continues: 'and thy Father which seeth in secret himself shall reward thee openly', the deep gulf between Buddhism and Christianity becomes apparent. As long as we are still influenced by the slightest thought of how God or the devil, who know of our conduct, might repay us, Zen would say; 'You are not one of us yet.' Actions resulting from such calculations leave 'traces' and 'shadows'. If a higher being is watching your actions, it will shortly call you to account. This is not the way of Zen." A good deed, according to Zen, leaves "no traces of smugness or self-glorification, much less any expectation of reward, even from God".

The Bhakti religion – which Rudolf Otto called "the most important rival to Christianity" – prescribes that religious belief must not be guided by any ulterior motive. It must not be the means to an end; above all, it must not be used to acquire wordly advantages. Selfishness is the sin of sins. The Puranas say: "Not to expect any reward, unending worship – that is the essence of true love."[12] If Christians try to convert Indians with the threat of hell-fire or the promise of heavenly rewards, they may be told: "Conversion for the sake of an advantage? Why, that is not religion at all, but its very opposite – selfishness. Our ancient Rishis teach us to love God for his own sake. That is true religion." Sri Aurobindo observed: "Let us give ourselves without reserve to the Divine. This is the best way to receive Divine Grace."

[12] *Bhagavata – Purana* III, 20, 14; quoted from A. J. Appasamy, *Christ in the Indian Church* (Madras, 1935), p. 91.

It cannot be denied that Christians tend to be selfish, sometimes even excessively so. Most of them would scarcely lead a devout life merely to please God. The thought of heaven and hell is often a decisive factor. But Asians, too, think first and foremost of themselves in their prayers and sacrifices. Even their supposedly unselfish devotion is rarely completely disinterested. In any case, a purely unselfish love is a deception. Consideration of one's own interest in devotion is not entirely objectionable. Self-seeking is sinful, but loving oneself is virtuous. The self, however, must be placed in God's hands. Man has no claim to worldly reward on account of his devotion. Christians generally expect blessings for living and acting devoutly. It is frequently claimed that a certain conduct will be "blessed" while another may be deprived of such "blessing", and "blessing", as a rule, is interpreted as worldly prosperity. Devotion to certain saints is supposed to guarantee protection. During the war, in a New Year's Eve sermon, a priest asked his parishioners to be of good cheer; their town, he said, was under the special protection of St. X. and thus would be perfectly safe. The following March, however, the town was destroyed by air attack, and many churches were burned down. The sermon did not sufficiently emphasize that Christians are not promised blessing and security on earth, that suffering is their portion.

It is above all in prayer that self-seeking is supposed to be evident. The pure worship of God unattached to any conditions, is more characteristic of Eastern Christianity than of its Western counterpart. Western Christians are less given to selfless prayer than their brethren in the East. Among Asian non-Christians, too, there are many who cultivate – or pretend to cultivate – an attitude of selflessness in their prayers.

Prayers, especially prayers to obtain favours, are most openly rejected in Hinayana Buddhism which holds that no superior beings exist who could help men effectively in matters of importance. Even Mahayana Buddhism which believes in superior beings and expects their help in many ways still has little understanding of prayers in our sense. I shall not discuss the higher forms of Hinduism. The core of the famous *Bhagavadgita* is contained in Krishna's words to the believer: "He who in all he does in life always remembers me, who loves me more than everything and has wholly surrendered himself to me, who hates no man and is attached to nothing, he, O son of Pandu, will in the end be united to me." Jiddu Krishnamurti wrote: "A quiet mind can never ask anything of God. It is only an impoverished mind that can beg, that can ask. What it asks, it never can have; and what it wants is security, comfort, certainty. If you seek anything of

God, you will never find God."[13]

The form of our prayers is not everywhere appreciated even in Islam. One of the prayers of the woman mystic Rabi'a (d. 801), whom Moslems remember with pride, puts it like this: "O my Lord, if I pray to thee in fear of hell, consign me to hell. If I pray to thee in hope of paradise, banish me from it. But if I adore thee for thine own sake, then O Lord, do not deprive me of thine eternal beauty."[14] When, during a Christmas service, Musharraf Moulamia Khan, a Moslem, was gently asked by a Catholic woman to submit his wishes to God, he thought: "Everything is known to thee. It is not for me to pray. Thou, O Almighty, all-powerful God seest everything." He added how difficult it was to stand in pure submission and gratitude before God, to receive whatever may be given to us like an empty shell.[15]

For Asians of this way of thinking, Western Christians are "traders" or "religious utilitarians", and their prayers are no more than "a mere bargaining, book-keeping by double entry with the deity",[16] an egoistic,

[13] *Krishnamurti's Talks to Boys and Girls* (Raighat-Benares, 1952), p. 64 et seq. See especially p. 68.

[14] See O. Karrer, *Das Religiöse in der Menschheit und das Christentum* (Freiburg, 1934), p. 60.

[15] Musharraf Moulamia Khan, *Pages in the Life of a Sufi* (London, 1932).

[16] See Sister Nivedita, *Die Hindu.* Romain Rolland, *Das Leben des*

"continuous insistent revolving round our own needs". So, we are told, our place is on a very low level of religion. Junyu Kitayama wrote: "Have we not transformed the wonderful altar of eternal creation into an abode of human weakness and sin? Have we not far too long kept God captive like a savage animal in its cage? We have treated him tenderly with low cunning, in order to let him know our desires." Old Indian writings reproach those who "want to milk virtue".

Prayers for material gain are a special object of Asian criticism. A Chinese once asked me whether we might pray to God for a prize in the lottery. Before I could answer, he told me the following story: "My mother was a devout Buddhist and often got up during the night to pray. She would open the window, put an offering on the ledge and pray to Buddha with folded hands. When I once asked her for what she was praying, she answered: 'For your health and prosperity, and an advantageous marriage for you'. 'But mother', I replied, 'you must not pray for things like that', whereupon she became very angry. Now I live among Catholics who pray much and go to church regularly. I have asked them, too, for what they were praying. The answer was: 'For success in business, for the prosperity of our children' etc. We ought not to pray for success in this world, but try to obtain it by our own efforts. We should pray only for things of the spirit."

Shripad Rama Sharma wrote in *Our Heritage and Its Significance*:[17] "India alone is the land where people, instead of praying for daliy bread – even when starved bodily, as they are today – meditate on the Gayatri, which means: 'I contemplate on the effulgence of the Source of all Light; let him illumine me.'

> From the unreal lead me to the Real,
> From darkness lead me to Light,
> From death lead me to Immortality."

Even Christians blame us for the selfish intention of our prayer. I know of Christians who have become Buddhists, because in Christianity they found a utilitarian attitude to prayer and its very opposite in Buddhism.

What we have already said applies also to this attitude. We may, even ought to, pray for ourselves and all that is necessary for our salvation. Material things may also be the object of prayer. But it must be remembered that God knows best what we need, and that we have no right to

[17] (Bombay, 1947), p. 61.

demand what does not contribute to our salvation. After the disastrous air raid on Munich in which the church of the *Herzog-Spital* was completely destroyed (April 25, 1944) the late Cardinal Faulhaber wrote: "From the ruins of this church we have to learn afresh that genuine prayer includes the absolute submission of our thoughts to God; that, though all the lights are threatened with extinction, the seventh petition in the Lord's Prayer – 'Deliver us from evil' – is preceded by the third: 'Thy will be done'. It is true that in the church of the *Herzog-Spital* prayers were said day and night without interruption, but for this very reason any superstitious concept of prayer must be discarded in the sight of these ruins. Those who pray must listen to the voice of him who speaks to us from burning bushes."

Moreover, these Asian critics ought to know that in the West, too, selfless prayer is not unknown. Goethe said on one occasion: "Great thoughts and a pure heart – that is what we should ask of God". There are, of course, innumerable Christians who think similarly, who in their prayers are mainly concerned with God and his Kingdom and who, when praying for themselves, ask for spiritual favours only.

After all, selfless prayers are the exception even in Asia, and "selflessness" in Hinduism and Sufism often has the

129

unpleasant implication that such freedom from desire merely conceals a vague consciousness of the irrevocability of fate, a false valuation of the created world, a lack of confidence in God the Father, who will be importuned by prayer and implored for our daily bread.

In Asia devout Christians, however, are blamed not only for their self-will and self-seeking, but also for "not minding their own business". Christians in the West rebel against many alleged and real evils in their midst, among their fellow men and in the world in general, and as a rule regard it as necessary and good to do away with these evils. They even believe in the possibility of stopping, or at least helping to stop them themselves. "Where there is a will, there is a way." Almost all Westerners put their trust in their mastery of the powers of nature, in self-education, influencing other people, social welfare, conferences, societies, reforms and the like. Even where the limits of thought and action and the need to fall back upon God are perceived, Western Christians are unable to get away from their own selves. Even then they think they know best, and only ask God to help them to change things but according to their wishes.

The thinking of most Asians runs along different lines. They are content with the world and its course, with God and his government, or at least resign themselves to it in their fatalism and belief in predestination. Indeed, to resist is of little or no avail. To be human is to stand helplessly before the tremendous forces of the spiritual and material world and of God. There is nothing left but humbly to obey. Buddhism goes even further in that it teaches the suppression of every desire and non-resistance to evil. Even in Japan there are similar ideas and sentiments. We tend to regard the Japanese as an active, busy people; but no other Japanese feature is so characteristic as the sudden surrender in a struggle and the relapse into apathy. *"Shikata ya nai"* – "What is the good of it?" a Japanese will ask in such cases. Not even Samurai education was able to obliterate this trait completely.

Many Asians, for example, the adherents of Hinayana and Mahayana Buddhism, go so far as to reject even their own self. Inspired by the Mahayana doctrine, Kitaro Nishida wrote: "Religious value means . . . the absolute negation of self. The ideal of the religious life consists in becoming a being that can see and hear without a self to see and hear. That is redemption." "Only by destroying the self", wrote Nishida, "is it possible to live in God." One has to reach a point "where there is neither 'I' nor 'God'". Sayings like these often have no other meaning than those of many well-known orthodox Christian mystics. It is therefore often only the language that is theopanistic, but not the thought and intention. Kitaro Nishida wrote: "We become a true personality by facing the wholly transcendent One." He thus showed how his words about the annihilation of the self are to be understood. Many Asians, it is true, believe in a real and complete annihilation of the self. These, of course, cannot understand Western concepts, seeing the personalities of God and man in sharp outline and clearly distinct from each other, and seeking to preserve man's own existence in perfection or in the state of beatitude. Here are fundamental differences between our thought and Asian Theopanism.

The eager outward activity inherent in Western forms of devotion bewilders many Asians. Some of our Christian services strike many Hindus, who see in God only tranquillity and immutability, as far too restless and disturbing. They demand a religious service which does not, with its ceaseless flow of words and chant, preclude the true silence for which they long. During the services in Gandhi's *Ashram* silence played a dominant part. Many regard the spiritual life of Western Christians as too restless. They always want to think, to desire, to feel, and to proceed from one point to the next. The Western Divine Office never dwells on any one thought, and cannot even do so. There is always some prayer in progress, aloud or in silence. There are no periods of complete outward and inner silence. Even in meditation there is no tranquillity. We are always driven to think, to make resolutions, to pray. In Asia, however, men like the fakirs are praised who are capable of stopping the circulation of the blood and dispersing and excluding thoughts and emotions. This emptiness is regarded as a value and an advantage. The Oriental wants to immerse himself in the well of nothingness and to escape from time. The *Gitansagraha* says: "Weary of multifold considerations and completely relaxed, absorbed in the deepest quiet, the sage forms no images in his mind, he knows nothing, sees nothing, hears nothing." Those who, fascinated by Laotse's quietism or the Buddhist methods of contemplation, have learned to appreciate tranquillity, silence and emptiness, will consider the movement and activity in our prayers and services as a lower form of devotion. Yet it is often forgotten that Western Christians, too, appreciate quiet, silence and leisure. They know forms of "nothingness" as, for instance, in Carmelite convents where "nothingness" and wholeness are sought. "Nothingness" means silence, detachment from material things, poverty. It is, as Edith Stein wrote, "a consciously and voluntarily pursued emptying of thought and will, of understanding and enjoyment, so that the presence of God may pour into this emptiness with unimpeded power and penetrate it, if one may say so, with a greater fullness". It is real emptiness, "an emptiness which has removed everything that is not God". That emptiness in reality is plentitude. "The great plentitude of great emptiness is the superabundance of his life."

Asians pray a great deal, but they would say with the Psalmist: "I will hear what the Lord God will speak in me" – "Audiam, quid in me loquatur Dominus" (Ps. 84:9). A sage has said: "Do not always address God, but be still and wait and let him speak to you. One word from God is more than a thousand of yours." That attitude is appreciated by Asians, while Western man is more inclined to speak himself. Asians prefer to listen. Our characteristic medium is vocal prayer; Asians prefer to be absorbed in God. Christianity, the "religion of prayer", has been compared with Buddhism, "the religion of contemplation and absorption".

The peoples of the East love meditation, but many of them look down upon Western methods of meditation. Suzuki wrote: "In meditation we have to concentrate our thoughts upon something, for instance, upon the uniqueness of God or his infinite love, or upon the transience of things. But it is precisely this that Zen wishes to avoid. Zen strives with all its power to attain freedom from all natural obstacles. Meditation is something artificially imposed, it does not correspond to the natural attitude of the mind.

The bird in the air, the fish in the water – what do they meditate on? The bird will fly, the fish will swim. Is that not enough? Who would wish to be bound to the unity of God or of man, or to the vanity of this life? Who wants to be disturbed in the process of his daily living by meditating upon the supreme goodness of a divine being or everlasting hell-fire? Seen from the viewpoint of Zen, the spiritual exercises and prayers of St. Ignatius are merely carefully elaborated products of his imagination. They are nothing but a heap of stones piled upon a man's head without any gain for his spiritual life. Yet many Asians, Christians and non-Christians alike, will feel attracted towards them, for different methods of contemplation obviously appeal to different people. Of course, the use of intermediaries in devotions is rejected by many Asians. Their slogan is: immediacy, experience and vision. Reaching beyond faith, all Buddhists desire higher states of consciousness and the experience of the Nirvana. The Hindu longs for communication and union with the deity in vision and experience. Hem Chandra Sarkar told me in Calcutta: "We are mystics. We see God." In short, they reject the priesthood as "une religion d'intermédiaires".

In the view of some the Western flight from the world and Western asceticism appear as an insult to God, since thereby the possibilities we have been offered are neglected.

In Tagore's eyes becoming a homeless ascetic *(sannyasi)* means to deny God who created the world. To escape from the world is identical with escaping from God. Though asceticism plays a large part in Asia, many Asians will, nevertheless, agree with Tagore. Many Asians do not see why some Christians consider the world and all its joys, such as married life, only as obstacles on their way to God. This prayer by Rabindranath Tagore illustrates their attitude:

"O giver of thyself, at the vision of thee as joy let our souls flame up to thee as the fire, flow on to thee as the river, permeate thy being as the fragrance of the flower. Give us strength to love, to love fully, our life in its joys and sorrows, in its gains and losses, in its rise and fall. Let us have strength enough fully to see and hear thy universe and to work with full vigour therein. Let us fully live the life thou hast given us, let us bravely take and bravely give. This is our prayer to thee. Let us once for all dislodge from our minds the feeble fancy that would make out thy joy to be a thing apart from action, thin, formless, and unsustained. Wherever the peasant tills the hard earth, there does thy joy gush out in the green of the corn, wherever man displaces the entangled forest, smoothes the stony ground, and clears for himself a homestead, there does thy joy enfold it in orderliness and peace."[18]

[18] R. Tagore, *Sadhana* (Munich, 1921), p. 183.

Christians indeed ought to hate the world and flee from it as well as to love it and use it as a passage on their way to God. They are not Manichees. *Per visibilia ad invisibilia. Per audibilia ad inaudibilia.* All created things can become the bread and wine of eternal life.

The use of imperfect and wrong means in religion is a common charge. Many Asians have no desire to reach God by way of spiritual exercises, prayer techniques, methods, visions, spiritual consolations and uplift. They prefer the cool clarity of "cognition" and reasoned mysticism. Others are repelled by the use of Latin as a ritual language and by the sacraments. A young Buddhist Singhalese said: "Christians tell me that they can approach Christ through the sacraments. But for us that is a physical matter."[19]

Many Hindus are embarrassed by the Protestant custom of receiving Holy Communion one after the other from the same chalice. The use of saliva during baptism disgusts them. Muslims hate the sight of statues and images in Christian churches. In their view painting is "idolatry of the eye" and music "idolatry of the ear". Works of religious art are considered to be dangerous and anti-God.

Many Asians are repelled by the way our devotional life is regulated and restricted. During the great Protestant

[19] *The Christian Life and Message,* etc., p. 144.

Missionary Conference in Jerusalem it was stated that "formalism in divine worship and church ceremonies" is the main obstacle to conversion for many Chinese.[20] The obligation to keep to certain formulas, forms and times has a similar effect. Sadhu Sundar Singh, with his leanings towards pietistic subjectivity, is certainly not an isolated figure in Asia. Western Christians are attached to a covered place of worship – the House of God. In the East prayers and meditation are more frequently held in the open. Asians believe, Junyu Kitayama wrote, that Western Christianity tries to capture God in magnificent church buildings. In the East, they would say, God may be found in solitary temples, on mountain tops, in the woods, in the cherry blossom and in the autumn leaves. In this respect Eckhart and St. Francis of Assisi are closer to the East. They are the builders of bridges from West to East. For they saw the real unity of God and the world. Junyu Kitayama wrote: "In the west God creates towers, churches, and cities; in the East, mountains, rivers, and gardens." This implies a misunderstanding of the Christian devotional life, but none the less it might be worth while to remember that our Lord prayed on the mountains and in the Garden of Gethsemane.

[20] *The Christian Life and Message,* etc., p. 112.

Large numbers of Asians appreciate the Western display of pomp in religious worship. But others, like Junyu Kitayama, interpret it as an attempt of Western Christianity to conceal God behind this splendour. The Japanese generally prefer a certain economy in the display of pomp. Sadhu Sundar Singh has little use for beauty in the liturgy. Catholic teachers in Wonsan (Korea) told me: "We prefer a simple service. It is easier to pray at Low Mass than at a Pontifical Mass." But Rabindranath Tagore showed his superior knowledge of men, including Asians, when he wrote: "A man who is strongly religious not only worships his deity with all possible devotion, but his religious feelings also demand expression in the splendour of temples and the rich ceremonial of the Liturgy."

With regard to the seasons, the East does not distinguish between the secular and the sacred to the same extent as the West. The difference between Sundays and working days is altogether unknown. In the West devotion is practically confined to certain days and hours. In the East, on the contrary, it is a matter of all hours and of everyday life. There is no difference between secular and religious life. The Asian mind cannot conceive of anything secular. Moslems, we are told, are pious every day; Christians only on Sundays, and then only for half an hour.

Nor is communal worship to everybody's taste. Until quite recent times the non-Christian Eastern religions have hardly had any communal services in our sense of the word: they were only introduced under the influence of Christianity. For a long time Asians used to object to the joint attendance of men and women in church. In many churches in China and Korea men and women were separated by a high screen in the aisle. Most temples are not even suitable for a common cult. What the East appreciates most is self-sufficiency. India is, indeed, the classical country of hermits. In the older forms of Brahmanism and Buddhism there is no common worship in the literal sense of the word; in Hinduism it is of minor importance. The people are in general content with *puja,* the private homage to the deity present in the temple and in the image of the god. The ideal is the ascetic with his solitary, silent devotion. Sadhu Sundar Singh did not care for prayer in common, but preferred quiet prayer at home or in the mountains.

Christian, and in particular European, devotion has also found recognition. Christianity has elevated and purified the piety of all the larger non-Christian religions and continues to do so. Hindus put less emphasis on the superstitious, idolatrous and immoral elements in their cults and are ashamed of their obscene practices. The Institute of Devadasis, it is true, still exists, but it has less importance. The Christian conviction that God is a spirit and must be worshipped in spirit has been widely accepted. Images of Christ exist in many Hindu temples, in Lamaist sanctuaries and in Japanese Buddhist teras. Even the Bible is read in some temples during certain ceremonies. Public services have taken their place side by side with private worship. Certain modern trends, like the Radhasvami sect and the Brahmo-Samaj, have been strongly influenced by Christianity and their services inspired by Christian forms of worship. These few examples go to show that our devotion has, at least in parts, made some impression on Asians.

Many sayings by Asians point in this direction. We know from the Islamic writer, R. Siraj ud Din, that devout Moslems are greatly impressed by the idea of private Christian prayer, by the simplicity and naturalness of public Christian worship, and above all by the family prayers which are quite unknown to Islam. In the Christian monastery of Tokwon a police officer told me that, when visiting pagans, he generally encountered bad temper and irritability, but Christians received him with a joy and cheerfulness quite incomprehensible to him. When soon afterwards he saw the monks at prayer, he said that now he understood that it was because of their prayers that Christians were cheerful.

Quite naturally Western forms of devotion are valued and respected by Asian Christians. Sadhu Sundar Singh found practical evidence for the truth of Christianity in the peace of mind conveyed by it, a proof against which thousands of books with the most powerful arguments were of no avail. Dr. John C. H. Wu, the Chinese diplomat and Catholic convert, extolled the supreme wisdom and spirituality of St. Thérèse of Lisieux as the fulfilment of what Laotse and Confucius had longed for.[21] Millions of Christians find in Christian piety what pagan religions are unable to give them.

[21] See *Beyond East and West* (New York, 1951); *Interior Carmel. The Threefold Way of Love* (London, 1954).

CHAPTER FIVE

MORAL AND SOCIAL ATTITUDES

In the East the conviction is prevalent that Western morality is far from perfect. Asians show a profound respect for the man who is prepared to make the supreme sacrifice and to give up everything for the sake of perfection, that is, for the homeless and naked saint. They positively demand from the religious man a maximum of heroism and renunciation. This heroism and even any serious moral effort, it is felt, are lacking in European Christians. Many regard Western Christians as too narrow-minded, too strict, but the majority think we are rather too easy-going and too slack. Western morality, as expressed in word and deed, in work and recreation, in the economic and technical spheres, in science and politics, in art and games, in the theatre and the cinema, is criticized as petty. Western Christians had never overcome evil and never would do so; they had become used to evil and come to terms with it.

143

A Japanese Catholic friend complained to me about the leniency with which paganism was judged by European theologians. He added: "Perhaps Christians demand so little from pagans, because they demand so little from themselves. A superficial acquaintance with the history of the Church will show that Christians are degenerate. They have become mediocre themselves, and in order to be able to defend themselves, they have made up fantastic stories about heathens." In examining the question why the work of the missions in Japan does not seem to make any progress, Father Totsuka concluded that the Japanese have their faults, but they knew the West not to be morally superior. Newspapers and films reveal the low moral standard of Westerners. That is a handicap to the missions in Japan. Totsuka emphasizes the fact that Asians from the Far East value virtue very highly.

Some Asians, however, have discovered in Western morality good and even admirable features. Khuda Baksch wrote of "European vices", but insisted that there were also "European virtues" (in particular, a spirit of co-operation, a high sense of duty, thoroughness, endurance). Kanso Uchimura, a widely travelled Japanese convert, censured the sins of the Christian nations most severely, but admitted their moral superiority. Among Christian nations, he maintained, public conscience exercises a beneficial influence, and youthfulness, liveliness and enjoyment of life predominate. Not a few Asians are drawn to Christianity through the example of Christian lives. The Japanese convert, Admiral Yamamoto, said that he was converted by the active, unselfish, and pious example of the Christian brothers.

Asians are fond of questioning the Christian character of Western Christianity. In this context they are thinking particularly of the Christian morality. They will say that it lacks harmony between the ideal and reality. There are gulfs which Christians had never bridged and were not able to bridge. I well remember the visit I received from the well-known Indian teacher Animananda in Calcutta, and his complaints. When he, who was certainly not a rich man and did not look like one, told people that he was a Christian, they looked doubtful: that could not be, they said, as he still owned certain things, clothes and the like. Christians, they would say, love wealth and are, as a matter of fact, rich. All Christians, including European missionaries, give most Asians an impression of wealth.

Moreover, Christians are told that they do not take seriously the decisive moral demands of the Sermon on the Mount; for instance, the demand to love their enemies, to renounce violence, to be absolutely true to their conscience, and to put infinite trust in God. Christians twist

145

the meaning of the commandments and try to get round them when they become embarrassing, jeopardize their life in the world, or require a decision. Asians take the Sermon on the Mount much more seriously.

Gandhi combined the utmost conscientiousness with supreme moral courage. The word "hatred" was lacking in his vocabulary. He had always rejected violence, having been inspired – according to his own testimony – by the Sermon on the Mount (Matt. 5:39). Among Christians Toyohiko Kagawa once showed what he meant by radicalism. When a young man told him he wished to become a preacher, Kagawa asked him: "Have you got the courage to go to prison, the indomitable energy to lead a strike?" "No. . . ." "Then you'd better give up the idea of becoming a preacher."

These charges contain much truth. Love of one's enemy is a rare virtue. Hatred abounds. The "God of Vengeance" can even be found in ecclesiastical pronouncements. A Protestant minister once remarked that neither Protestants nor Catholics had really been converted to Christianity. A European Catholic country priest said that his peasants were still pagans. They meant well and would certainly go to heaven – but they were not Christians. These verdicts are too harsh, but it is true that many Christians are as yet inwardly anything but Christian.

Our life and actions are held to be lacking not only in Christian characteristics, but even in ordinary morality. Ku Hung Ming declared: "The peoples of Europe have, for the greater part, lost their understanding of the power and sacredness of the medieval civilization. They are not yet sufficiently advanced in the new civilization to use it as the dominant factor in the maintenance of civil order. So at present they have to be kept in order not by some kind of moral force but by crude physical force. ..." Others have gained the same impression.

The objections to Western moral motivations are closely related to objections to Western devotions. The Bhagavadgita, one of the most famous sacred Hindu scriptures, proclaims as its ideal, not man's flight from the world, but the fulfilment of the duties allotted to him. This has to be achieved, however, without selfishness, "without attachment", not for the sake of gain or merit, and thus, like all genuine morality, it requires humble surrender (*abhyasa*) and the renunciation of all worldly interests (*vairagya*). In the view of many Asians this ideal is superior to the Christian, for in the moral sphere Christianity makes use of the motives of merits and rewards. The condemnation of Western morality is, of course, not universally shared by all Asians. Many will recognize genuine morality in the West. Indeed not all consider the motives of punishment and reward in the sense of the Gita.

The charges, however, go further than this. Christians are said to be lacking in what is truly human. In China Europeans used to be called "the barbarians from the Western Isles". These conceptions are not yet completely dead. Western scientific and technical achievements are, of course, known and admired, but at the same time it is asserted that through science and technology men have become alienated from themselves and have lost their human dignity. Many Asians regard Western civilization simply as a delusion, as a "refuse of industry and the machine and a caricature of true culture". In Chinese eyes, the Westerner appears capable as a scholar, a technician, and a soldier; but he is regarded as inconsiderate and lacking in refinement of the heart, a barbarian.

Sun Yat Sen said many years before the Chinese Communist regime was established: "There is nothing more crude, more brutal, more malignant, than the present civilization of Europe and America. It can be summed up in two words – aeroplanes and guns. We Chinese call this barbarism." When, during a visit to the beautiful Malayan island of Pulo Pinang I asked two Indians, a merchant and a newspaper editor, for their opinion about European civilization they answered, "It is only a special form of barbarism. It is true, you have more railways, more factories and machines than we have, but you have no souls." And Rabindranath Tagore spoke of the "systematic dehumanization" of Europe.

The West is troubled about many things

In the East the individual is generally of little importance. Physically and spiritually the individual is a limited substance or even *maya*, at least inferior insofar as it is individual, finite and isolated. The individual being only "exists" within the universal and divine being. Above all man, as Junyu Kitayama points out, is not the centre of the world. He is not even privileged among other creatures, but like them he has to carry the universe. Everywhere in the East suprapersonal values, ties and communities are of greater importance than the personality itself. We are indeed separated from the East by the value we attach to the individual soul, the original personality, the genius. The wisdom of the community, the caste and the nation are more valuable than individual knowledge and analytical research; care of the community more valuable than care of the individual.

Goethe's dictum that personality is the supreme happiness of mortals would therefore in the best of cases hardly provoke Asians to more than a smile, while Hegel's doctrine of the personality as sovereign and centre of the world would leave them perplexed. The Western cult of the personality, its self-confidence, and egocentricity, are complained of everywhere. In the West the whole has to serve the individual. Through the improvement of social conditions, only the development and welfare of the personality is to be served in the long run. But all this, Asians feel, is wrong. Western ideals like "liberty" and "equality" are also repudiated in the East.

It cannot be denied that among large sections of the European population the personality is respected and cared for at the expense of the community. Indeed, we would admit that the happiness of society requires a reduction of individualism and a greater consideration of community values and suprapersonal ties. The man who regards himself as the "be-all" and "end-all" of life will never reach perfection. Yet, on the other hand, we would insist that every man and his soul are of infinite value, that the individual is nothing and yet something great, that, as Pascal said, "man infinitely surpasses man". In our view the proper social order is one in which the rights of the community are so bound up with those of the individual that, in the words of Balmes, "they neither eliminate nor encroach on each other". In Asia, the individual has few rights. He is only slowly gaining them – under the influence of Christianity, or losing them where Communism rules. Rabindranath Tagore praised Europe for having brought Asians "the ideal of moral freedom", for being the standard bearer of "freedom of thought and action", of "freedom of conscience"[1].

The East disapproves of the emphasis on developing the personality as much as on the cult of personality. In general, the whole of man is 'formed' in Asia, even a member of the lowest castes and classes carries a certain dignity 'like a toga'. The European is regarded as immature. In his efforts to organize the world, it is said, he forgets to develop his outer and inner self. The informal behaviour of Americans is, in the eyes of Asians, sheer barbarism. Lack of dignity is the mark of Western man.

Western superficiality is held to be a symptom of this lack of maturity. Westerners, Asians say, are completely dominated by their search after distractions and pleasures. Even thought and research are concentrated almost entirely on the visible world, not at all, or too little, on the spiritual. Indians may say: "You people in the West set out to conquer the visible world, whereas we in the East

---

[1] Rabindranath Tagore, *Nationalismus,* p. 114 et seq.

have for thousands of years been exploring the invisible one." Vivekananda said: "For the Hindu God and the soul are the only realities infinitely more important than the world." Others say the West may have "scholars" but no "sages". More than a century ago, the Japanese Hirata Atsutane (1776–1843) wrote in his book, *The School of Dutch Science:* "Their eyes are glued to the futilities of the material world; but they have no comprehension of the sublimity of the great gods. Their teaching is thus narrow and limited." That has remained the judgement not only upon the Dutch, but upon the West as a whole. In our day, however, Asians themselves turn increasingly to materialism.

Western man is also said to be lacking in harmony, the pleasing unity in diversity. He is unable, one is told, to adapt himself harmoniously to all given conditions. Japanese women, for example, dress according to their age. Young girls wear clothes in bright, cheerful colours; old women dress in grey. They thus keep their ethical sense in the choice of their clothes according to their age, wrote Nyozekan Hasegawa, while European women try to simulate youth even in old age.

Onesidedness is also quoted as proof of the Western lack of form. The spirit is developed at the expense of the body, the intellect at the expense of intuition, knowledge at the expense of the will, work at the expense of the inner self, or vice versa. Sri Aurobindo held that Asia, like Greece and Rome, "exalted art, poetry and philosophy and valued ... her social organization ... inordinately". But she "valued more highly and worshipped more intensely her saints and religious founders, her thinkers and spiritual heroes".[2]

Some forms of this onesidedness, such as the exaggerated emphasis on physical fitness, are particularly obnoxious to Asians. Everything, it is said, is done for the body – to the detriment of the soul. The athlete is honoured rather than the saint.

Asians have little sympathy for the Western craze for work. The European, we learn, is essentially a worker or even a slave to his work, and work in factories, offices, and barracks is nothing but slave labour. Rabindranath Tagore compared the "whole man" of Asia with the "economic man" of the West. He said that civilization, although boasting of its love of freedom, created worse forms of slavery than had ever been practised in human society. Man is so bound up with the mechanism of work that he has no freedom left. There is no time for necessary recreation. Junyu Kitayama calls our perpetual restlessness the

[2] *The Message and Mission of Indian Culture.* Extracts from the writings of Sri Aurobindo. Compiled by J. Sen (Pondicherry), s. a. 7.

scourge of the West. It was the fate of the West to pile achievement upon achievement. In the East, he said, natural growth is regarded as the purpose of life. The whole idea of time is different. In the West where only the man who works is respected, old age and gradual loss of strength are the worst fate that can befall him, whereas in the East it is graced by a new beauty, as a last chance of enhancing human dignity. Our restlessness is also criticized especially in big business, industry, politics, research and technology.

Eastern people love to rest blissfully when they have reached their goal, like the river that finds rest in the ocean. Western man seems to Asians like a mountain stream always rushing towards new quests. Western man lives in a world of incessant activity and empty noise. He even wishes to live like that and is afraid of contemplation, which shows that he lacks true wisdom and spirituality. Chinese and Indians will reflect that they have learned their lesson from great catastrophes, as for instance the collapse of Aryanism in India or the Hoangho floods in China. Europeans, on the other hand, still have to learn that real "progress" can only take place in the mind. A Chinese proverb runs: "Action is easy, knowledge difficult." Rabindranath Tagore said: "The only genuine progress of man is synonymous with an expansion of his emotional range." Lytton Strachey tells the following characteristic story of Florence Nightingale in *Eminent Victorians*: "At one time an Indian admirer, the Aga Khan, came to see her. She elaborated on the marvellous progress in the administration of hospitals which she had lived to see with regard to drainage, ventilation, and improved sanitary installations of all kinds. After a pause in the conversation, the Aga Khan asked: 'Do you believe that you are on the way to becoming a better person?' She was slightly puzzled, and asked: 'What do you mean by "becoming a better person"?' 'To have more faith in God', he replied. She noticed that his idea of God was different from hers. After the conversation she entered in her diary: 'A most interesting man, but he has no idea of sanitation.'"

Doctors in a German hospital told a Korean colleague about their day. Work in the laboratory began at half past six in the morning, operations followed, then visits of the patients and so on till the evening. Then the Korean asked: "And when do you think?" Dr. Hsiao was more positive. He remarked that Westerners differed from the Chinese in that the Chinese were calm while Westerners in their Faustian urge were pushing forward unceasingly, though they were well aware of the limitations of their energy and abilities. This was the cause of much evil. In China inventions had always been developed to a certain stage only, whereupon they were suppressed. In the last resource, the Faustian urge of the ever dissatisfied Occidental was a gift of God and must be used. But God does not want man to search only outside himself. In this respect, too, man must learn to be humble, or he would lose his head.

We have already mentioned the problem of time. Despite his awareness that life is short and the world a transient thing, the Asian has always time and will never allow himself to be imprisoned in a strict daily or seasonal routine. On the other hand, Europeans never have any time: "watch-in-hand" is their characteristic attitude. Every single minute must be used. Days, weeks, months, and years must be strictly ordered. We can barely afford a real holiday, for even then trains are running and machines are working – things that Asians find strange. They have sufficient time to enjoy life, family, friends, leisure, religious rites — and indeed time itself.

In 1932 an Englishwoman, Mrs. Weir, wanted to show the Dalai Lama what progress her sex had made and told him, as a proof, that Amy Johnson had flown so quickly from England to Australia that she had broken the record set up by men as well as women. The Dalai Lama considered the matter for a few seconds. Then he asked in astonishment: "Why was she in such a hurry?"[3] On the

---

[3] *The Tablet,* December 28, 1946, p. 356.

other hand, the present Dalai Lama showed himself fascinated by Western technical achievements, such as photography, when he met Heinrich Harrer.[4]

These criticisms are combined with complaints about the destruction of oriental civilization through this craze for work and restlessness. "Like the trunk of the mythological elephant, the chimneys of Manchester have for a century been swallowing the treasures of the seven civilizations of Asia", wrote Falih Rifki Atay, a Turk, a hundred years ago.

These accusations are not entirely unjustified. But the "ceaseless progress of action" only started in recent times and is, as has been rightly observed, more characteristic of Protestantism than of Catholicism, of Calvinism rather than Lutheranism, although here one must not generalize. Not every European or American works as hard as the Asians think.

The above-mentioned Falil Rifki Atay on one occasion ridiculed the English weekend. God, he said, worked six days and rested one. However, the English rest two days a week. In London every week-end a migration lasting forty-eight hours took place. If an Englishman were told on a Saturday afternoon that war had been declared, he

---

[4] Heinrich Harrer, *Seven Years in Tibet* (London, 1953).

would answer: "We'll talk about that on Monday."
Nations like the Germans, who work harder than the
British, were unpopular. They were thought to have no
savoir vivre and to want to disturb the order of the world by
their industry. Yet in Japan and in China people work still
more than in the industrial countries of the West. Besides,
the "calm" and "leisureliness" of a great number of Asians
is, as a matter of fact, based on their love of pleasure.

Many Asians are astonished at Western irritability and
pity us for it. Asians are proud of their equanimity in the
face of adversity and blame Europeans for rebelling when
faced with disaster. In the Brahman of the Upanishads, in
the Nirvana of Buddhism, calm and tranquillity is the
supreme note. The ideal of the Hindu is equanimity and
peace. The Buddha of Kamakura, smiling serenely, represents to the Asian an ideal superior to the bustling activiy
of Western Christians. Some maintain that irritability is
the basic Western sin. A native of Sumatra, who watched
a missionary losing control of his horse remarked: "The
man has no breeding."

Equanimity and patience are indeed among the main
characteristics of the Asians. As early as 1583, A. Valignano
wrote of the Japanese: ". . . They will allow no word of
abuse, not even when it is uttered in anger. Even with
employees and workers of the lowest grade, we must

speak politely since they will not resist bad treatment.
. . . They are very patient, more than seems credible, and
unruffled in disaster. . . . Even in the depths of misery they
appear to live in such calm and lack of anxiety as if they
had lost nothing. . . . In their passions they are equally
moderate, so much so that they do not display them to
the outside world, even though they may feel them."[5]

I have never seen an agitated Japanese. Neither earth-
quakes nor wars can throw them off their balance. If once,
however, their calm is upset, the effects are terrible. The
Japanese is then inclined to violence. The Chinese, too, do
not lose their temper easily. Again and again wars have
devastated their country, their fields have been ravaged,
and their cities and villages laid in ashes. But as soon as the
war is over and the last soldier has gone, work starts at
once. In Pulo Pinang I was told of Chinese who accepted
the change from wealth to the greatest poverty with
profound equanimity. Suddenly impoverished they started
the very next day to earn their living as coolies. The wife
of the revolutionary, General Aguinaldo, in the Philipines
described patience as one of the most characteristic ideals
of the Filipino. Nothing better could be said in a man's
praise than that his calm was not to be shaken. She said

[5] A. Valignano in his MS. *Sumario de Japon*.

that any haste especially in the religious sphere, for instance when saying Mass, was considered repulsive.

In many cases the indolence of the Burmese is actually touching. Whatever may happen there is sure to be something to laugh at. If a fire starts, as it frequently does, nobody thinks of fighting it. Everybody laughs at the grand joke and their laughter is joined by the victims. When a British consular official, who was bathing in the river, took umbrage at being watched by the natives, and by their laughter and chatter, they said: "Master, we were only waiting to see what happened for yesterday a crocodile caught one of our men."

R. Siraj ud Din, a convert from Islam, wrote: "Self-control in unimportant matters can make a lasting impression (on Moslems). A Moslem convert to Christianity once greatly impressed me. He was preaching when one of the audience took the Bible out of his hands and disappeared. But the preacher showed no sign of irritation."

Asian equanimity is proved even in the face of death: it is accepted as a matter of course. The aim of Japanese education before the war was to train the pupils to be at all times prepared for death. During a great famine in India people would rather die than slaughter the innumerable cows which roamed the country. But discipline and self-control are also the essential qualities of the Christian character.

Western restlessness and its craving for work are considered by Asians as evidence of materialism. All Europeans, they say, are materialists at heart, all prefer material values – money, possessions – and sensual to spiritual pleasures. It has become a platitude to speak of Eastern spirituality and Western materialism. According to Gandhi everything that the West had given to India was infested by "satanic" materialism. Upadhyaya Brahmabandhav believed that a disastrous materialism had engulfed Western civilization, and all nations infested by Europeanism would be driven together with it to utter ruin. As a remedy against materialism Asians recommend their spirituality and equanimity. Ku Hung Ming announced in his book *China's Defence Against European Ideas* that the materialism of Europe and America can and must be overcome by the morality of China.

Europeans reject this general accusation of materialism. Jacques Maritain in *Reflections on America* maintains that Americans are the least materialistic among the modern peoples which have attained the industrial stage, nor are Americans egotistical. One could hardly find another nation as generous as Americans are with their money for charitable purposes. In their basic aspirations the United States are a deeply spiritual country. Maritain wrote: "If a new Christian civilization, a new Christendom is ever to

161

come about in human history, it is on American soil that it will find its starting point."

It is hardly fair to call the European spirit materialistic because it developed a materialistic civilization. The blind Egyptian Taha Husain (b. 1889), whose autobiography is a literary masterpiece, emphatically denied the purely materialistic character of our European civilization. He wrote that Europeans were not materialists, because they continued to make great sacrifices in the service of science and the mastery of nature.[6] Huh Shih called such superficial comparisons between the materialism of the West and the spiritualism of the East a "myth". On the other hand, Asia and its religions are not free from materialism. In many cases even Asian devotion contains materialism in disguise. Père Lachin was told by Chinese: "The Chinese people want nothing but to eat, to drink, and to earn money. All the rest is literature." Moreover, materialism is steadily gaining ground in Asia. "The torrent of the modern mechanistic business spirit", wrote Suzuki, "mercilessly floods the entire East, scarcely leaving a quiet corner to which one might retire for meditation. Soon even the solitary island of Zen will be swallowed up by the floods of common materialism. Even the monks already begin to mis-

[6] See J. M. Abd-el-Jalil, *Brève histoire de la littérature Arabe* (Paris, 1943), p. 292 et seq.

understand the spirit of the early masters". In China Communism is a determined and brutal champion of materialism.

Westerners are not only criticized for their materialism but also for their love of pleasure. John C. H. Wu wrote: "We people of the East endeavour to reduce our desires to a minimum; the people of the West continually seek to improve the means of satisfying their desires." A young Chinese told me that his father had impressed on him the need of hard study. In Europe, he was told, young people must enjoy themselves and live to the full. That seemed wrong, for youth is the time for study. Man passes away swiftly like a rocket. Then dark night closes in again. Love is only one shoot on the tree and not so important as all that. Work, achievement, and the preservation of the family are far more important.

Social Problems

According to Asian opinion Christian society in the West is even more defective than the individual Christians.

It is said that the West had not succeeded in permeating social life – business life in particular – with the Christian spirit. An Indian told me: "I have heard many foreigners call their civilization Christian. That is nonsense. The civilization of modern Europe is certainly not Christian in spirit. . . . Has Europe really been Christianized?" Among the important social virtues, which the West is held to have realized only insufficiently or not at all, are truthfulness, loyalty, justice, mutual understanding, and charity. Tao-Pung Fai wrote that it was rare to find any genuine love of one's neighbour among Western Christians. In support of his notion that modern Europe was not dominated by the spirit of God, but by the spirit of Satan, Gandhi after the First World War referred to the absence of love of one's enemy. "The last war has proved more clearly than ever the satanic character of the civilization which dominates Europe. The victors have broken every moral law in the name of justice."

Western social ideas are said to be very dangerous for the East. This is a complaint which even some Europeans and Americans may support. An American professor of divinity at the Protestant Missionary College in Tsinanfu told me that, in spite of the best intentions in their missionary work, the effect of individualism and liberal ideas had been disastrous. These ideals should not have been applied so precipitately. The schools had produced Bolshevists. J. S. Gale, a Korean missionary with a profound knowledge of the East, said: "Contrary to our intentions we have ruined the Far East by undermining the relations between children and parents, between the sexes, and by introducing socialism ."[7]

Many Asians do not understand the superior and free position of women in the West. In the East they are subordinate to men not only in Islamic, but also in Buddhist and Confucian areas. The Japanese woman used to have a superior position but lost it under the influence of Confucianism. This is shown in the famous codex of morality, *Onna daigaku,* edited by the philosopher Kaibara Ekiken (d. 1714). Even in modern Japan a woman has to serve her husband and children. She does not share their meals. She has to follow the man and in trains the husband will sit down before his wife does.

To the Asian mind the public activities of European woman are an unprecedented anomaly. In the East women live on principle in greater retirement than in Europe. God and nature, it is said, have destined the home as their place. As a rule they live a cloistered life in Zenana or Harem and do not appear in public, especially not in temples and mosques. Women are not even mentioned in conversation. Many oriental love-songs are addressed to boys and not to girls. In Confucianism, Islam and other religions at least the external manifestations are reserved for men.

[7] J. S. Gale, *A History of the Korean People,* p. 196.

The Japanese Yuri Sugimura once complained about the way Western travellers, writers and missionaries wrote about Japanese women. According to their reports Japanese women were little more than slaves and toys of their menfolk. They were supposed to have little education, no high ideals and no rights. They were superstitious, ignorant, morally weak, degraded and unhappy. Condemned as they were to service, they had not much to enjoy in life. But these travellers were looking at everything from the point of view of their own race and religion. I am happy, she said, that I was born in Japan in the simple, clean atmosphere of Eastern civilization. Women must work in the West as well. Does that make them happy? Happiness is a state of mind and not necessarily dependent on luxury. Japanese women for the greater part are busy at home; they do not travel, they do not go into politics or go in for social welfare work; but probably we are happier than American and European women with their freedom. The reason is quite simple: We are happy because we sacrifice ourselves in order to make our children and husbands happy.

Recent events, above all the last war, have led to changes and given women a position in public life. In Siam, where women have always enjoyed greater independence, they fought as soldiers and a voluntary women's force was formed. Women labour forces are a characteristic feature of the new Communist China.

Coupled with complaints of the public activities of Western women are those of Western disregard for the family. The Turkish writer Nahit Sirri Iltan (b. 1894) described the French woman as elegant, charming and witty, but without any respect for honour and family life; Turkish women, on the contrary, were homely, unpretentious and good housewives, faithful, willing to do everything for their husbands. Indian merchants often spoke derisively to me about the white women they had met; they lived only for pleasure and had no interest in any real purpose in life.

Lax sexual customs – even the free association between the sexes among Europeans – and flirting and dancing are regarded by many Asians as extremely scandalous. It would be impossible for an Indian woman to dance with a man who is not her husband. I was told by a Chinese that a man may hold out his hand to his sister-in-law only when she is in danger of drowning. He remarked seriously that it showed the difference between man and animal. *Time* magazine reported on July 11, 1946: "The inhabitants of Chunking believed that woman's place is in the home, that no pretty girl would be seen with a man in public, that only a prostitute would play and drink with a man, and that marriages were arranged by the parents only. The American Army employed many Chinese girls who had been brought up in sea-ports under European influence. The crowds spat at these girls who arrived with the Americans and threw stones at them, so that they had to be protected. The city authorities sought to explain the situation by telling the people that Americans were odd people, accustomed to talk and go out with women."

In Japan no loving couples can be seen in public, no indecent films are displayed. Kissing in public is thought unbecoming. The Chinese consider a kiss something "voracious".[8] According to Lin Yutang, a kiss is "one of the things Chinese dislike . . . kissing on the screen, on the stage, at the station, and goodness knows where else". An Indian told me during a voyage that his people failed to understand the freedom of relations between men and women to which Westerners are accustomed. He said that he lived only for his wife, she only for him, and that in his shop in Manila he kept at three yards' distance from every woman. He was shocked that European men approached women, and women approached men they did not know. The way in which European women dress is regarded as provocative and shameless. Christians in the

[8] See A. E. Crawley, "Kissing" in *ERE,* vii, p. 740.

Far East are also very strict in these matters. Common services, in which men and women participate, proved one of the most difficult problems for the missionaries at the beginning of the modern age.

Indescribable poverty, greater than any European can imagine, is to be found in the countries of the East. What has been achieved in the field of social welfare is minimal; much more could be done. The individual plays a less active part in the struggle with misery than he might, either because of fatalism or innate carelessness or submission to the will of God. The Indian Bhils have a saying: "What pleases God is right." Hence there is no understanding for the comprehensive social welfare services of the Europeans. Others, it is true, praise Europeans for fighting against misery. Rabindranath Tagore, for example, extolled the West for "employing all the forces of mind and reason in order to heal the sick and alleviate the misery to which we submit in hopeless resignation". A gigantic attempt at combating this resignation is being made in India to-day.

It is almost generally deplored that social organizations are considered important, whereas the natural communities which the Asians regard as sacred and divine are ignored and even left to die. Rabindranath Tagore spoke of "the road to suicide" pursued by the nations of the

West, "who choke their humanity under the terrible weight of their organizations in order to keep themselves in power and others in slavery". On the other hand, he had to admit: "We must not deny that there is in the West a living soul – perception of which cannot be completely discarded – engaged in silent struggle with the huge organizations under which men, women and children are destroyed because their mechanism is ignorant of spiritual and human laws."

Criticism is also levelled against the Western pattern of the family. The way in which marriages are contracted is said to be wrong. Asians find it difficult to grasp how men can so easily meet women in the West. In the East the will to marry and support the woman is always presupposed. It is equally inconceivable that the man himself chooses the woman and vice versa. K. Ogata's remark that the young man does not yet possess the wisdom and maturity necessary for the choice of a wife represents the conviction of Asians. In their opinion, the wish of the young people must not be the only decisive factor, otherwise divorces and other evils may result. The family as well as tribe, people and state have an interest in the marriage. "What matters", wrote the Japanese K. Ogata, "is not the personal and even sometimes doubtful and transient happiness of individuals, but the continuity, the immortality of the family and at the same time the dignity of its tradition." An Indian merchant from the Punjab told me: "When in India a young man has reached marriageable age, his parents and relatives choose a girl for him who is suitable by virtue of her background, character, inclinations and other circumstances. I am bound to love such a girl – though I may have never seen her – whom my parents are selecting with so much care, my parents who only want the best for me and must know better than I do what is good for me."

Many people in the West seek in marriage mainly the satisfaction of their sexual appetite. Asians, on the contrary, desire above all to have children. I have heard of a Korean Catholic who, as his first wife was unable to have children, married a second one for the sole reason that he wanted above all to have a family. The prevalence of polygamy is best explained not by sex but by the desire for offspring. Ku Hung Ming wrote: "The customs of China make it the primary duty of women not only to live for their husbands, but to watch over the name and the heritage of the family."

Western Christians are told that they have not been successful in raising, sanctifying and transcending sexual life. Always and everywhere it is covered by dark shadows. The Western attitude to celibacy is regarded as significant.

171

A London Parsee explained to me that for them an unmarried man is a frustrated man. Ku Hung Ming compared celibacy with non-resistance; it had no moral power and would never be a suitable remedy for social evils. "When the world is bad the Buddhist will shave his head, enter a monastery and boycott the world. But in this case the bad world will only go from bad to worse and finally reach the point when it will burn down the monastery together with its shaved inmates." Nor can the East understand why so many Westerners evade marriage. "We are still in the habit of marrying our women. We all want to marry. In America I observed the exact opposite", said an Indian.

With regard to sexual matters, many Asians adopt an attitude totally different from the Western. The Upanishads perceive in "mutual pleasure" *(samarasa)* a potentiality for the experience of the inexpressible One, the blessed identity. For the Hindu, the sexual act is a "religious act". The begetting of a son is the main duty of every Hindu. For the Narayana sexual pleasure is a sacred act. There is hardly a non-Christian religion in which the cult of the phallus does not play a part.

In the Catholic view all sexual life suffers from the consequence of original sin. But Catholics will have to admit that they have not done their best to consider sex as something willed by God, and to fight the "desecration" of a God-given instinct. "We have allowed the source of life to be desecrated. The fire of love is not bad in itself; a slavish yielding to passion is."[9]

The appreciation of human beauty and sexual love are only rarely regarded as steps on the way to the love of God. For many Western Christians religion and sexual love, Agape and Eros, are enemies. In some Eastern religions this is quite different.[10]

Many Asians are shocked by the frequency of divorce in the West and the facility in obtaining it. In the East, marriage is widely regarded as a sacrament. The wife must be faithful to her husband until death and even beyond death.

Asians are also put off by relations between children and parents in the West. Objections are raised to the coming of age of Western children. This is an example of a particularly marked contrast between East and West. A Chinese told me: "My father is and always will be my father. I may be sixty years of age, but all the same, I owe him reverence and obedience. When I enter his home, I must greet him reverently and wait humbly till he gives me permission to speak or to do anything. My father once

[9] See B. Griffiths, *The Golden String* (London, 1954), p. 41.
[10] See Th. Ohm, *Die Liebe zu Gott in den nichtchristlichen Religionen,* pp. 418, 420, 467.

said to me: 'Even if you have grandchildren, I shall still be entitled to box your ears if you should do wrong'."
The Chinese added that, in his view, it is a sign of egoism and ingratitude for grown-up children to leave their parents, who had done so much for them and needed them in their old age.

The high praise given in the East to a child's loyalty finds its explanation in the position of the family. In China and Japan twenty-four examples of loyalty are put before children, the following among them: Once upon a time, there was a boy who had a stepmother. She was quite heartless especially to him. The boy, however, was always out to please her. Once in winter when no fish was available of which the stepmother was very fond, the boy laid himself naked upon the ice until the warmth of his body melted a hole through which he was able to catch fish for his mother. ... A son slept naked by the side of his parents in order to attract the mosquitoes and prevent them from disturbing his parents' sleep. ... Roraishi in his seventieth year dressed in children's clothes, babbled like a small child and crawled on the floor to give his parents the illusion that they were still young.

It is not surprising, therefore, that Chinese and other people from the Far East find some passages in Holy Scripture hard to understand or even scandalous, for example, Christ's saying that he had "come to set a man at variance against his father and the daughter against her mother, and the daughter-in-law against her mother-in-law" (Matt. 10:35); and his words: ". . . Who is my mother, or my brethren? . . . Behold my mother and my brethren! For whosoever shall do the will of God, the same is my brother, and my sister and mother" (Mark 3:33–5). That is what the Chinese find difficult to accept.

This applies also to other sayings of Jesus. A former Chinese Christian wrote: "These Christian doctrines are as little suited to our mentality as the head of an ox would be to a horse's body. Only think of it! The cardinal virtue of the Chinese people is respect, and principally respect towards our parents. Yet Christ teaches: 'Whosoever loveth father or mother more than me is not worthy of me.'" Adherents of Confucius have considered Jesus as a dangerous person because he counselled his followers to leave their father and mother and told them: "Let the dead bury their dead". But it may be pointed out that Christ himself belonged – and wished to belong – to a family, that for many years he lived and served in a family, that he used the family as a simile for what we are to expect in the Kingdom of Heaven; in one word, that his attitude to the family was positive.

In their valuation of the clan Europeans and Asians differ widely. In Europe the small family is the general standard. Western text-books on ethics and law do not concern themselves with the clan. How very different is Asia where independent small families are the exception. The small family is merged with the clan, that is the community of all those who are descended from the same father. Even after marriage a man remains a member of the joint family which absorbs him and his wife and children. The independence of small Western families is not understood, but held responsible for many evils. It is more incomprehensible still that some people sever their family ties completely and work only for their own profit. If in an Asian family there is a single wealthy man or one who earns a comfortable living, he has to look after all the other members and he will do so, and it would never occur to him to refuse; for that would be an offence against the divine law. Therefore even poor people are not afraid of having large families; for there will always be someone in a position to protect the family. The sense of mutual obligation, of the subjection of the individual to the family, is universal and extremely powerful.

Racial problems have hitherto been relatively unimportant in Asia. Hardly anything was known about them.

A change came with the arrival of Europeans and their racial consciousness. Over and over again the European idea of racial superiority has hurt the Asians and roused their indignation. Rabindranath Tagore, who regarded Christ as "the great leader of mankind", said that by instituting racial differences Christians had been the greatest sinners against the brotherhood of men. The treatment of racial problems in the colonies has scandalized Asians. To quote Tagore again: "From the very beginning India has tolerated different races, and she has shown this spirit of toleration throughout her history."[11] The European powers, however, embarked on discrimination – "they who themselves came as strangers to countries which they now dominate."[12] In cases where the European powers admitted foreigners to the colonies, they reduced them to slavery and made them undertake the most menial tasks.[13] We can sympathize with these complaints. But Hindus themselves ought to remember their treatment of Parias and of the aborigines of India. The attitude towards Goans and Pakistanis is a blot on modern India's record. Asia, too, has sinned and is still sinning against other races. We might instance the struggle between the

[11] Rabindranath Tagore, *Nationalismus,* p. 143.
[12] Ibid., p. 143.
[13] Ibid., p. 146.

13*

dark-skinned Dravids or Tamils and the light-skinned Singalese in Ceylon, which led to mass murders in July 1958.

During the last decades Europe has shown an extremely active interest in the conception of nationality and the problem of nations, that is, groups that are united through certain characteristics such as common settlements, language, traditions, or customs. National consciousness and, even more so, Western nationalism has up to now constituted a stumbling block to many Asians. Mankind was considered of greater importance than one's own people, and the true perfection of a nation consisted in the subjection of selfish interests to the great spirit of mankind.

Unfortunately this attitude is mainly theoretical. The average Asian has always cared most for his own family. The Chinese used to show concern only for his family, not for the nation, still less for mankind. Despite our sins and failures Asians could have learned much from us in this respect and, indeed, have done so. Europe has taught them, as Rabindranath Tagore wrote: "Besides our duties to the family and the clan we have higher duties to mankind in general."[14]

Western nationalism is the feature in our national life which is most unpleasant to Asians of the older type.

[14] Rabindranath Tagore, loc. cit., p. 114.

They know nothing of national differences, they are scarcely familiar with the idea of a nation. "In general Asia is of a universalist, not of a nationalist cast of mind." Islam, in particular, is by its very nature hostile to nationalism. Said Halim Pasha, in his manifesto *Islamization* described nationalism as anti-Islamic, and despite the upsurge of nationalism in the Near East, there is a widespread longing for the great supra-national empire of the Caliphs. Confucianism has always laid particular emphasis on humanity. Kaibara Ekiken, the philosopher of Confucianism, said: ". . . We are all brethren, since we are all sprung from the womb of the earth."

Motivated by this spirit, Asians reject the European apotheosis of "nation" and "state". Where they prevail, men and the human community are made to suffer. Tagore expressed his opinion in words to this effect: In the West mankind is, by the national mechanism of trade and politics, properly compressed in bales which have their uses and high market value; they are clamped with iron bands, labelled and sorted out with care and accuracy. In reality, however, God created man that he might be human; yet this modern product is fashioned with such wonderful regularity and so highly polished that the Creator will find it hard to recognize it as a spiritual being, as the creature he made in his image. Another passage is as follows: In the so-called free countries the majority of the people are not free; they are driven by the minority towards an end unknown to them. In the words of Said Halim Pasha, nationalism imprints its local characteristics on religion and thus disfigures and violates it.

Asians certainly overlook that nationalist ideas have unfortunately exercised a magnetic attraction on them. In Shintoism they themselves have raised patriotism to a religion. They forget that to-day extreme nationalism is condemned by Christians everywhere. For them, as for Tagore, Chauvinism is "a terrible epidemic". The Catholic ideal is an universalism which accepts and includes national individualities.

Many Asians criticize the way in which religion is excluded from politics in many Western countries. In the non-Christian empires of antiquity there was a close connection between religion and the state. That was true of the Christian Middle Ages as well. Luther was the first to give up the principle of subordinating secular government to the Church. This led to a complete separation of Church and State. Religion was confined to the sacristy or to the privacy of the home.

In Asia the old idea still prevails. As we have already shown, religion embraces everything, and everything is religion. Even politics and the state are part of religion.

Religion is and must be totalitarian. In Japan there is a slogan, *Saisei Itchi* that is, identity of politics and religion. Baron Hiranuma, a former Japanese Prime Minister, remarked: "Finding out the will of the gods, that is politics." The emperor of Japan rules by divine commission.[15] In Islam religion and the state are identical; religion and political life cannot be separated. The Koran also applies to the life of the nation and the laws derived from it govern secular as well as religious and ritual questions. Ibn Saud said: "They (the Arabs) must be educated according to the will of God. . . . You cannot govern people without religion. . . . I have had machines imported from Europe, but I will have nothing to do with irreligiosity." Ghandi once confessed, "Most religious leaders I have known are politicians in disguise, while I, who wear the mask of a politician, am at heart a religious leader." For Ghandi, religion had priority before politics. His actions were not determined by any prospects of success or considerations of prestige, but by religious and moral principles. In him religion and politics had become one. In Communist states the old ideas still prevail; they are totalitarian and demand a corresponding ideology which is a pseudo-religion.

[15] Not to be taken in the sense attached to "by the grace of God".

It is on account of this totalitarian approach that Asians misunderstand us. They find it hard to believe that the separation between state and religion is an actual fact in the West. Not even missionaries are always believed when they say that they have no political aims, because this was sometimes different in the past.

Asians disapprove of Western politics because of its lack of morality. In the life of the nation a moral standard different from that of private life prevailed. There should not be a double morality.

Public life in the West is also censured for its lack of spirituality. Rabindranath Tagore held that Western nations were not bound together by spiritual values, but by a purely mechanical "organization for commercial and political ends", "the organized selfishness of a people".

A popular target for criticism are the power politics of the West. Rabindranath Tagore called the power of Europe an evil thing. Satan himself, he declared, serves European civilization; but Europe would not remain unpunished. The terrible furies it unleashed against God's creation would turn against Europe itself.

The blessings which the West has brought to other nations, especially non-Europeans, are only rarely mentioned, yet these are many. Among them are the abolition of the slave trade, the ending of the continuous wars among primitive tribes, the protection of many poor people against exploitation, the struggle with disease, severe measures to prevent suttee and the murder of children. They must not be forgotten when the imperialism of Europe and its black record are mentioned. One should remain objective as some Asians are.

It is said that the way in which force and war have been used by the West is a mockery of all that Christianity means. In the old China war was considered as of the devil and the profession of the soldier universally despised. An old Chinese proverb said: "Good iron is not used for making nails, nor are good men for making soldiers." In the fourth century B.C. the Chinese philosopher Moti said that war showed the greatest lack of universal love. In modern India the Ahimsa commandment with its injunction to spare all living beings and its stress on all-embracing love, is still held up as one of the most important commandments.

Hsu Shih regarded the "martial spirit", which is basically a love of adventure, a characteristic feature of the European. Europeans enjoy competition, going to war, and they are trained to obedience and the readiness to fight and die for impersonal ends. All this, however, belongs to an inferior order.[16] Hei Lung describes the West as

[16] *The Chinese Renaissance* (Chicago, 1934), p. 14.

suffering "from an over-estimation, even an over-breeding, of the hero type". No other nations, it is said, have fought so many wars as the Christian countries. However, Asians can hardly claim that the spirit of violence and war is lacking in their own history. Power has always been an instrument of politics and the numbers of Asians are increasing to-day who have put their faith in power politics. This tendency is very noticeable in India and, for instance, in the Indian attitude towards the problems of Goa and Pakistan. Moreover, Western Christians might have grounds for refusing to be held responsible for the acts of violence and war committed by their own nations.

The Christian faith condemns the glorification of the State, power politics and the morality of the "doublethink". Christians are not to blame that power politics have prevailed. Such apologies will not, however, convince Asians: it is precisely their own failure, one is told, that Christians have been unable to realize Christianity and to penetrate the state with the spirit of Christianity. They have allowed domination through violence to invade Christianity, they have bowed to Christian imperialism, and attempted to enforce their Christian ideals with arms.

Particularly popular arguments against European Christianity are the suicidal massacres and mutual destruction during the last war. These above all are taken as evidence of the bankruptcy of Christianity or Europe's defection from it. Ibn Saud once said: "Hatred does not stem from God. Europe, impregnated with hate, will destroy itself with its own weapons!" To-day, on the other hand, there seem to be many Asians who criticize Western Christianity precisely on account of its rejection of heroism, conquest, power politics and extreme nationalism.

Subduing Nature

Asians differ in their views of our attitude to nature according to race, religion or individuality. Inclined as they are to illusionism, dualism and universal pessimism, they find it hard to understand the deep esteem with which we treat *maya,* the visible universe. Respect for money, wealth and private property is rarely to be found in the East. The world is only an empty shell, a dream and a delusion. True reality is hidden beneath the veil of the material world. Genuine wisdom is to be found in men like Buddha of whom a Brahmin in the days of Akbar said: "He had the ultimate courage to see no colours where our longing paints the world in colours."

Those who have a primitive-animistic, a sublime theopanistic or cosmic-mystical attitude to the world and to nature marvel at the West. The Japanese have no conception of creation, no supra-natural, sharply de-

185

fined idea of a personal God. For them, God, nature and man merge into one, and they are thus at one with nature, with God-Nature. Nature means very much to them, it is an object of worship and of sublime aesthetic pleasure. According to Junyu Kitayama, a basic attitude of the Asian spirit is to believe in the cosmic relation of all things. These are not divided by differences of size and quantity. A large proportion of Asians actually regard nature as part of the deity, and man, himself belonging to nature, also as part of the deity. *Tat tvam asi.* This feeling of universal oneness generates reverence for nature in her creative power and beauty, love of all her creatures, and joy in contemplating her. The Japanese are fond of observing nature and treat her with respect. They even spare the life of old trees.

All who think and feel in this way will be shocked by the Western habit of looking at nature, its attitude towards it. Nature is attractive to Europeans in a purely sensual way. Yul-gok, a Korean author of the sixteenth century, wrote: "When scholars visit the Diamond mountains, they frequently observe them only with the eyes of their bodies, forgetting that the soul within should look as well. The spirit of God desires to demonstrate his will through all this." Western man is governed solely by a matter-of-fact outlook. He has no reverence for what is 'below him' in nature. The Faustian urge to subdue nature and the world is significant. He is incapable of attaining to a truly spiritual enjoyment of nature.

Asian criticism of the Western attitude towards material things runs along similar lines. They are said to take up far too much space in his life. He indulges in a shallow optimism, based on the idea of continuous progress through his inventions and organizations. In Asia to adapt oneself to nature and the world, to endure nature, to yield to the supreme will which works through nature is rightly regarded as the highest virtue, the supreme ideal. Europeans pay little attention to the origins or ends of nature, to its meaning and destiny and treat it arbitrarily and insolently. "The West seems to be proud of having subdued nature; as though we were living in a hostile world in which everything that we need had to be wrested from an alien and spiteful order of things."[17] Things, however, had taken their revenge. For in reality man is dominated by matter, matter is not dominated by man.

Such generalizations contain a grain of truth. Far too often and grievously has man forgotton that nature is God's creation and has its own significance, that it does not exist only for his sake and that he tends to violate it.

[17] Rabindranath Tagore, *Sadhana*, p. 9.

The Western attitude to animals must be mentioned. The Ahimsa-commandment in Buddhism, Jainism and Hinduism, the commandment of "not killing" or "not doing harm" is valid not only for human beings, but also for animals. The Jainas shrink from killing even the smallest living creature. Indians see in the inclusion of animals in the Ahimsa-commandment a proof of the superiority of their religion over Christianity. The Ahimsa-commandment, they say, is superior to the Christian commandment of love. A Chinese told me that our habit of eating meat presupposed that we made animals suffer. Chinese found that hard to understand. One of the reasons that prevented Gandhi from becoming a Christian was that in Christianity he missed charity towards all creatures. Bhai Manilal C. Parekh[18] argued that the Gospel account of the Gadarene swine proved that in his evaluation of animal life, our Lord did not rise above the ethical standards of his time. A Chinese asked me whether people in the West realized that the eating of meat involved pain for animals. An Indian blamed Christ for not having proclaimed a third commandment to love lower animals.[19]

Western man is even accused of a wrong attitude towards plants. The cursing of the fig tree which is related in St.

[18] *A Hindu's Portrait of Jesus Christ,* p. 393 et seq.
[19] O. M. Buck, *Our Asiatic Christ,* p. 72.

Mark 11:20–5 is supposed to show lack of respect for trees. In Indian eyes, trees and animals have a life which ought to be respected. It is thought that in this respect Christ was not in advance of his time.

Christianity, too, demands charity towards animals. For a Christian all cruelty to animals is sinful. But on the other hand we cannot agree with the Indians who on principle make no difference between animals and men.

Rabindranath Tagore foretold that "the clumsy edifice of modern progress" cannot last for long. The collapse is inevitable. After the conflagration, however, the eternal light of the Eastern sun, "which is destined to bring light once again to the whole world", will rise "in the East which saw the dawn of the history of mankind". But there are still moral forces in the Western nations; morally Europe is not finished. Christianity still exists and will continue.

CHAPTER SIX

CUSTOMS AND USAGES

CUSTOMS and usages are time-honoured and binding traditions of society. They are the sum of all the rules and
laws which govern life and action in a community, family,
clan, tribe, nation, class, neighbourhood, village, city, and
the Church. Such customs keep the individual within the
bounds of his community and its tradition.

The customs of Christians or of Christian communities
have not the same intimate, lasting, and essential relationship with Christianity as the moral law has, but are,
nevertheless, important because they train the Christian
in a manner compatible with Christianity; they give
his moral and religious life an outlet, motive power and
support. They are also important for the impression and
the effect of Christianity on non-Christians. Christianity
has countenanced or produced the customs of Christian
countries and can be judged and valued by them. Many a
European missionary has discovered that his European
manners made his work difficult or even impossible.

Especially important are the customs in the Church
which pervade her entire life and colour the views

which non-Christians have formed of Christianity.

In the East, tradition is all-embracing; everything is regulated down to the smallest detail: eating, drinking, social life. The formality with which Japanese salute each other would strike us as amusing, and the Japanese tea ceremony would be well-nigh unthinkable here. The free-dom with which Western man moves in the world, in his home and in church, makes a strange impression on many Asians, the impression of informality and lack of neatness. Our customs are actually in a state of decline. Modern times have contributed much to their disintegration and thus to the breaking-up of our communities.

Customs are extremely strict in the East. Manners are determined by unwritten laws. Offences against them are not treated lightly. This is another reason why Asians find European behaviour strange.

Church customs are looked upon as being European and contribute much to the fact that Christianity as a whole is regarded and rejected as something typically European.

Many Indian, Chinese and Japanese customs may make Europeans laugh, whilst others strike them as repulsive. In popular lectures on an Asian country the speaker often dwells with relish on these things. On the other hand Asians find many Western customs ridiculous, or even foolish and barbarian. Thus our table manners strike many Asians as quite funny and lacking in common sense. Nearly everywhere in Asia, whenever opportunity arises, people like watching Europeans at their meals. Their remarks are not always flattering. They cannot understand why we do not use our washed hands instead of spiky, sharp instruments like knives and forks.

Western hygiene is regarded by Asians as inferior. Japanese and others find it strange that we keep handkerchiefs in our pockets – in Japan paper is used instead and thrown away after use – and that many Europeans have baths only rarely and go to bed without washing.

Some features of Western social life, gestures and figures of speech strike Asians as odd. Asians are much more formal than we are and have a surprising wealth of social convention. Their marks of respect are numerous and varied, strictly graded in accordance with the degree of relationship, age, sex, rank etc. of the parties concerned. In this respect, Europeans are actually impoverished. Asians find it disagreeable to shake hands or even kiss in public. To enter houses and churches with the same shoes that one has worn in the street is regarded as lack of manners.

There are some special liturgical practices which shock and repel Asians as, for example, the use of saliva in baptism and the questions addressed to the woman at the marriage ceremony.

CHAPTER SEVEN

RELIGIOUS ART

ALL that is and is not beautiful in the West is known in the East. Rabindranath Tagore was familiar with the "smoke and dirt" and all the "ugliness" with which machines and warehouses "disfigure a beautiful earth". In his opinion Western industrialism had sown "a poisonous seed of physical and moral hideousness over the whole earth".

He wrote of the clumsy, gigantic industrial organizations: "The mere fact of their ugliness shows that they are out of tune with the whole of creation. . . . Beauty is the seal set by the Creator on his creation when he is satisfied with it. . . . If your commerce does not share the dignity of beauty it is false."

Here we agree with the poet. Truth goodness and the divine are beautiful, and real beauty is true, good and divine. The beauty of a thing permits us to draw conclusions as to its dignity and value. All the ugly sights in the West are indeed signs that men have been estranged from

God. Yet ugliness in the West to-day is not the fruit of Christianity but of a de-Christianized world and civilization.

The buildings that were put up in the East as well as the West during the nineteenth and early twentieth centuries seemed strange to Asians, and yet they were attracted by them. Soon they showed the desire to build and possess similar buildings. There were individual Europeans and Asians who objected to this alien type of architecture, but their protests went unheard. The copying of Western models has continued despite all complaints about Western influences. Taken as a whole traditional Asian architecture is a thing of the past. Contemporary buildings are to be found almost everywhere and the once magnificent old city of Peking is to-day characterized by modern buildings.

Some sensitive Asians are in no way blinded by the novelty and strangeness, the size and pompousness of much modern architecture; they advocate that it ought to retain its local character. It should certainly meet the needs of our age, but at the same time preserve contact with the past.

Until recent times few Asians have understood Western painting, which is not surprising in view of some of its strange forms as compared with their own traditions. Islam forbids altogether the representation of human beings. Other religions permit it, but subordinate man

194

to nature. Only recently have artists in the East begun to paint nudes. Much of Western sculpture is rejected in Asia. Moslems do not allow the representation of the human body. Indians choose the most mobile shapes for their gods. Yet the tendency of modern European sculptors to go back to the inspiration of primitive art forms, to simplicity and vitality, has made new approaches possible between East and West.

European music had always been thought barbaric in the East. An Indian friend, hearing some opera singers practice in his neighbourhood, asked what the reason was for their moaning. Old men from the Bataks hearing the missionaries chant asked them: "Why are you weeping?"

Europeans can hardly expect to impress Asians of good taste with their dress, which, compared with the dresses of civilized Asian nations, is lacking in taste. If they are imitated at all, it is because they are practical, cheap and happen to be European or American. People want to keep up with the West.

Great Christian art is not unknown in Asia, but Asians also see Christian art which is not worthy of the name. Christianity is rich in magnificent achievements in all fields of religious art. These are mainly achievements of the past, however, and the modern decline in religious art has been noticeable almost everywhere. Strength, originality and inspiration have gone. There are no great modern works of art. Old patterns and subjects have been varied. Consequently churches and homes are filled with objects of religious art that dishonour the religion they are supposed to glorify.

The missions are in the same plight. The Christian mission in Asia was at the height of its expansion when Christian art was declining in Europe, the home of the missionaries. In general no artistic value is attached to the churches which have been built in Asia, or to the paintings and sculptures, to the vestments which the missionaries introduced, or to the dances that took the place of the old sacred dances. Much of it is paltry compared with Asian architecture, painting, sculpture and vestments.

These facts may well cause a sense of shame and bewilderment, for they prove that there are shortcomings. Art indicates clearly and mercilessly the degree of truth, value, dignity, splendour and purity that a religion contains. Apathy and blindness to true beauty, the absence of desire for it, inferior art do not commend a religion. It is not entirely inconceivable that people should conclude from present-day religious art that Christianity is dying or is dead. At any rate, the art of the turn of the century has little to recommend Christianity. In spite of this, Christianity can still boast of an infinite wealth of beauty in

literature, in the liturgy, in painting, sculpture, and architecture. There are indeed indications that the lowest stage
in the decline of art has passed. Yet to-day in the
West there are churches, sculptures, paintings and vestments which deserve the name of art. Even in the missions
the lowest point has been passed. Practically everywhere
there is indigenous Christian art of a high quality.[1]

Moreover, the present stage of religious art should not
provide the only criterion by which to judge Christianity; it
should be taken as a whole. Art is an important measure for
the assessment of a religion, but not as safe as many people
think.

There is need to discriminate between Christianity in
general and Western Christianity in particular. Fortunately
– or is it unfortunately? – Asians have taken little or no
notice of the weaknesses in Western art. On the contrary
they are attracted and impressed by much of it, especially
by ecclesiastical buildings. The missionaries always point
to the taste of the masses as an argument in favour of
church buildings in the European style; but there are also
many who think differently. Cardinal Costantini, one time
apostolic delegate in China, wrote: "A well educated
pagan, accustomed to the beauty of the vestments in his

[1] Cf. A. Lehmann, *Die Kunst der Jungen Kirchen* (Berlin, 1955);
S. Schüller, *Die Geschichte der christlichen Kunst in China* (Berlin, 1940).

country, cannot but be repelled when he sees the ordinary chasubles in our churches." The liturgical colours in Roman Catholic churches strike Asians as unpleasant. In the Far East white is the colour of mourning and of death, red the colour of brothels. Consequently newly purchased red rugs had to be removed from a Japanese church. Some Japanese explained to me that Christianity would have to be "japanized" also with regard to church fittings and vestments. Red and black were not suitable colours. I was told in Tokyo that a Japanese who had been invited to Pontifical High Mass in Sekiguchi remarked afterwards: "It was quite nice, but not a patch on our Buddhist ritual." The missionaries have every reason to banish ugliness from their churches and from the liturgy, and to develop a sense of beauty in all aspects of Christian life. They ought to study the views of those who possess a sense of beauty and are kept from embracing Christianity by what is ugly in it. Beauty in the last resort is rooted in religion and contributes to its influence. It can express what logical arguments never will. It reveals the invisible behind the visible, the inaudible behind the audible, the movement of the spirit behind the movement of the body. Beauty is a criterion of truth. It ennobles and transfigures man. It leads him to God. "Aesthetic appreciation, certainly at its highest and best, seems to open a window from some spot of here and now into an eternal world, and carry one beyond what the eyes see or the ears hear. The aesthetic method is much closer to the religious type of life than is the scientific method."[2]

[2] *Report of the Jerusalem Meeting of the International Missionary Council,* i (London, 1928), p. 299.

CHAPTER EIGHT

THE CHRISTIAN MISSIONS

An investigation of Western Christianity must include the world-wide Christian missions, for hitherto they have been mainly the responsibility of European and American Christians and were directed from the West, with chiefly European and American missionaries. There have always been Asians who were friends and patrons of the missions.[1] There have always been Asians who considered missions as good, a source of blessings and even necessary. Often enough Popes, bishops and Christians have been asked, even implored to send missionaries.

But there have always been enemies of the missions in Asia as the history of the persecutions proves. In some countries these have lasted for centuries and only abated about a century or so ago. Meanwhile they have started again. Many thousands suffered martyrdom for the faith during the last centuries, even during the last decades.

[1] See the study by the Indian Uraon, Simon Bara, "Aboriginals and Missionaries" in *The Light of the East Series* (Ranchi, 1944).

The Christian missions have never been criticized as severely as to-day.[2] There is now an organized, systematic criticism of missions. The Indian Nyogi Report is one of many examples.[3]

Innumerable Asians maintain that there is no justification and need for Christian missions at all. They point to the present state of Christianity. "Why have missions?" they ask, as Paul Hsiao tells us. "The Christian nations are no better than we are."

A Chinese who had given up his Christian faith asked: "Why should the old leaven, which has long since ceased to be good enough for you, be imported into China? We are about to do away with all that is obsolete – not with all old things and to build something new. Why should we not replace it with something quite new?" Missions, they believe, imply the rejection of all other creeds and a violation of the spirit. They are unjustifiable and foolish, senseless and inhuman. In Gandhi's view missions are "an intrusion into the sanctity of the personality". "Every mission" he wrote, "runs the risk of falling into a 'religious imperialism', dangerous to itself." From his point

[2] See K. M. Panikkar, *Asia and the Western Dominance* (London, 1953). Also J. D'Souza, *Sardar Panikkar and Christian Missions* (Trichinopoly, 1957).
[3] Published in 1956.

of view any conscious attempt to convert others by means of more or less rational arguments was an abuse of reason itself. The end desired ought to be: to make Christians better Christians, Moslems better Moslems and Hindus better Hindus.

The missionary can only reply that Christ instituted the missions, that he has a sacred obligation. "For woe is unto me if I preach not the Gospel" (1 Cor. 9:16). Gandhi's protest against the missions was based upon a mistaken conception of religion. He advocated the fatal idea of a national religion conditioned by race and place. He was once asked whether Christians might be permitted to work at least among African cannibals and animists. The great Indian eventually realized the validity of these and similar objections.

In his book, *A Hindu's Portrait of Jesus Christ,* Bhai Manilal C. Parekh deals with a passage in the Gospel of St. Mark, where the apostles tell Jesus that they forbade a man to cast out devils in his name because he did not follow him. Jesus replied: "Do not forbid him" (Mark, 9:38–40). "In this rebuke of Jesus there is a great lesson for Christians for all time. They have monopolized the name of Jesus and the spiritual life it connotes for their own individual churches, and have not hesitated to close the gates to heaven against all who would not come to him through their little doors. Christian missions have followed this monopolistic policy to a very large extent, and they have often been most jealous of those who would approach Jesus directly."

The aim of Western missions is also criticized. Many Asians will only accept missions which help the peoples of Asia to rise from their misery and destitution. They reject those that aim at conversions and wish to turn non-Christians into followers of Christ. Every man should keep to the religion to which he belongs.

As a matter of mere statistics Asians will point out that the missions have had very little success, in spite of all their efforts and all the money spent. Hardly any Moslems and Hinayana-Buddhists have been converted. That was a sign of the weakness of Christianity and its missions. On the contrary large Christian territories had been lost again, among them former Christian strongholds like Asia Minor. The Moslems tend to say: "So many Christian nations have already become Moslem, but it has never happened that a Moslem nation has become Christian."

One of the chapters in Panikkar's book, *A Hindu's Portrait of Jesus Christ,* is entitled "The Failure of the Christian Missions" and deals with the "failure of the Christian attack on Hinduism, Buddhism and, of course, Islam". The results of the missions are "disappointing in the extreme". "Asians will continue to develop their marked individuality and remain spiritually and intellectually apart from Christian Europe."

Those who have been won over, it is said, have been no gain, for they have come almost entirely from among the poor and destitute, the peasants, and the illiterate classes. In China, for example, Christianity had spread almost only in the country areas. The missions had not been able to make much headway among the city populations, nor did those who were converted lead very different lives afterwards.

To concentrate the missionary effort mainly on children might be advisable, but among adults no real change of heart was achieved – so the argument runs.

Yet figures in themselves prove nothing for or against Christianity. Christ himself had only a few apostles and disciples. In addition the successes of the missions are not as insignificant as is assumed. In face of all the difficulties with which the missions have had to cope, especially in Asia, their successes must be described as astonishing, not only with regard to numbers, but above all with regard to quality. The large number of martyrs gives evidence that many Asian Christians take their Christianity seriously. Besides there is also a fair number of Christians among educated Asians.

In a former chapter we mentioned the evil consequences which, in the opinion of some Asians, are the result of Western missionary work, such as the decay of religion, the decline in morality, etc. In the words of Tang Luang Li, the missions have contributed "to a high degree to the disintegration of the national community and the spirit of the people".

These charges are either exaggerated or false. The disintegration of many ancient communities and religions is a fact, but the missions are by no means solely or even chiefly responsible for this. The same would have happened – perhaps even worse – without Christianity and without the missions. Many old social systems and religions are breaking up, whether Europeans and Asians like it or not. Some aid must be at hand, and in such times of transition Christianity has the resources to help all those who would be helped.

Other charges are levelled against the method used in missionary work. Western missionaries, it is said, do not wait for the Asians to come to them of their own accord, but pursue them and try with great zeal to convert them. "For the charity of Christ presseth us" (2. Cor. 5:14). The native clergy, at least the Catholic clergy, do not do this. Almost everywhere in the East, I was told, native priests are better equipped for the preservation of the established order, better suited for pastoral care than for conversion work. They are not particularly active. Europeans are more suitable for real missionary work. Only recently, in 1958, a Hindu Christian from Kerala complained that the native clergy were after money, gave themselves airs and were out of touch with the faithful. Missionaries from abroad were still most likely to win the people, but on the whole the zeal displayed by European missionaries meets with disapproval.

This attitude is not completely unreasonable. Not all native priests show the zeal of missionaries from the West because that is not their way. Rabindranath Tagore met two ascetics in a village and inquired about the particular features of their teaching. "Why do you not preach your doctrine to all men in the world?" – "He who is thirsty will come to the water of his own accord." – "But what about it? Do you find that happening? Do they come of their own accord" – The man smiled gently. Without the slightest sign of impatience or anxiety he answered with confidence: "They must come down to the last man." Gandhi thought that religion was best propagated by the noble lives of the faithful. "The rose stands in its own place and spreads its perfume."[4] Missionaries should live like Christ.

[4] D. S. Sarma, *Studies in the Renaissance of Hinduism in the Nineteenth and Twentieth Centuries* (Benares, 1944), p. 573.

The methods of European and American missionaries meet with the most serious criticism. Asians will put up with the fact of their preaching, but less with the manner in which it is done and least of all with their fight against non-Christian religions. They are believed to condemn these creeds without even knowing them sufficiently, to make incorrect statements about them and then to spread these misinterpretations. An example is the "worship of idols". But no Asian worships idols. There is talk of "polytheism" where there is none. The proof that these deities have no power consists in demonstrating that they are unable to help; but neither do the Christian's saints give any help. The lack of tact and forbearance, or consideration for other religions is held against the missions.

It cannot be denied that many missionaries condemn other religions and oppose them, without being familiar with them. Some treat these religions with contempt and make a caricature of them. A well-reputed missionary in Trichinopoly (India) acted on the principle that pagan religions must be shown to have not a single redeeming quality, otherwise we should meet with no success. In a text-book of Catholic religion entitled *Tchu kio jo tji* (Seoul 1906), we read on page 15: "All words in Buddhist books are false and frivolous and contain nothing worthy of belief." This is both shortsighted and wrong. Missionaries ought to be objective in all circumstances, even if this makes the work more difficult. Perhaps such an attitude is more realistic and virile, however, than soft-pedalling all differences and flying from the truth. Neither Buddhism, Hinduism, nor Islam is a religion willed or instituted by God. It has been pointed out that for historical and psychological reasons religious reformers have rejected or even been forced to reject altogether the religions or faiths they were fighting, but this will not do as an answer to Asian charges.

The struggle against the non-Christian religions is criticized as much as the actual process of Christianization. The missionaries are said to argue people who have no judgement of their own into accepting Christianity. As though it were impossible to accept Christianity after due reflection and in full freedom. Not infrequently missionaries are told that they had certainly built up 'a wonderful mechanism in the technique of mission work', but had failed in the spiritual and religious spheres. That was why they resorted to schools and hospitals in the service of the apostolate. Western Christians will be told that Buddha won half of Asia without the resources commanded by the West. Gandhi had the greatest influence without almost any organization. It may be that the West expected too much from its material impact from schools and hospitals and too little from spiritual values and proper religious methods.

The use of money and other gifts has discredited much of Western missionary work especially among the upper classes. This was, and still is, a particularly vulnerable aspect of missionary methods. I will only quote what a more modern book has to say about the mission among the Bhils. People used to speak contemptuously of "rice and rupee Christians". Some declared quite openly: "We accepted baptism for the sake of the money." One convert remarked he had accepted Christianity "in order to satisfy his hunger". French missionaries in the Bhil missions had been accustomed to spend money lavishly in order to help Christians and to support and enlarge the missions. When some years ago this mission was taken over by the Missionaries of the Divine Word they discontinued this practice – for lack of money, but also for reasons of principle. The first effects were shattering. Great bitterness ensued and even defections; but the missionaries stuck to their new policy and it was soon accepted.

A very popular accusation was that European missionaries were always supported by their own Governments, but this is no longer the case. There are, or were, Christians and missionaries who even condoned certain types of violence, but nowadays no Catholic missionary would or

15*

could use violent methods, quite apart from the fact that the Catholic Church explicitly repudiates any use of force in her apostolate.

Missionaries are frequently blamed for introducing Western forms of Christianity and Western methods. Unfortunately, this is largely true. It is only lately that foreign missionaries have learnt to adapt themselves to their surroundings, besides being gradually replaced by native priests. In many Asian countries a native hierarchy has already been established and there are three Asian cardinals, an Armenian (Agagianian), an Indian (Gracias) and a Chinese (Tien). Christian architecture, painting, music, liturgical vestments and forms of devotion are being adapted to Eastern traditions.

The Western ability for adaptation is often disapproved of. Pagans believe that such methods of adaptation are only employed in order to deceive them; Asian Christians, on the other hand, are against adaptation because they aim at a new and different order. Christianity in their eyes means war against the old order which must not be covered up.

Efforts to attract young people are a cause of much discontent. By the spoken and written word and in their practice, Western missionaries often advocated the idea that nothing much can be done with old people, and that they must get hold of the young. Members of the former

Scheutveld China Mission explained to me that older people were not really changed by conversion. Consequently they staked all their hopes upon the young and the children of the newly converted; hence the importance of schools was emphasized. To the Asian mind, however, this seemed like capitulating before the difficulties of adult conversions. Missionaries have rightly been blamed for this attitude also by Western Christians, because it showed no confidence in the power of the spirit and repudiated the force of Christ's message. Finally, we mention a criticism of a fundamental attitude of the West. There are Asians who appreciate Christians and especially missionaries because of their devotion, their zeal and their efficiency, but they miss one thing – joy and the radiance of a smile. Westerners seem so serious, so tense, so strained. They are not relaxed. This may or may not be so. However, O. M. Buck is right in saying: ". . . joy is its own argument and proof. A radiant face is Christianity's noblest and most unanswerable apologetic. Anything less than joy is shattered by controversy. India and the whole world await once more a message of deep joy, that is a well of water springing up unto eternal life."[5] It is in this sense that this author regards the future of the missions dependent on the contagious nature of joy.

[5] O. M. Buck, *Our Asiatic Christ*.

However such critical voices are off-set by those who favour and even praise Western missionary methods. Hem Chandra Sarkar, president of the Sadharan Brahmo Samaj, told me in Calcutta: "We welcome the Christian mission. The missionaries do a great deal of good." Various Asian governments invite and support the work of the missions. During the last war the Japanese governor-general of Korea visited the Benedictine Abbey of Tokugen and told the monks that they had nothing to fear and might safely continue their work. The government knew well what they meant to the people. Simon Bara, who belongs to the Uraon tribe, which had suffered much under the Hindus, wrote: "We venture to maintain that genuine religion has been introduced among us. Education and reforms are carried out tactfully and in accordance with scientific principles." Rai Bahadur Sarat Chandra Roy, a lawyer, a devout Hindu and founder of the magazine *Man,* mentioned the "phenomenal progress" in education among Indian aborigines thanks to the missions.

The most powerful impression is made by the charitable activities of the missions which have almost miraculous effects. Never has there been anything like it in the pagan world. Even within the different Asian peoples, charity had achieved very little. In the past, nobody cared for anyone outside his own family; and suddenly, strangers from far-away countries came to relieve suffering in Asia! Paganism has nothing to match this. The inhabitants of Sumatra told their missionaries: "You are merciful; that is something of which we know nothing."

On my extensive travels I witnessed repeatedly the profound confidence and great love of Asian Christians towards their missionaries. A Japanese scholar, K. Kato, wrote in *The Psychology of Oriental Religious Experience,* that the decisive factor in conversion is "the respect for the Christian character of the missionary, for a life indicative of a wealth of affection, kindness and manliness". Rai Bahadur Sarat Chandra Roy, a Hindu, praised the missionaries for their "life of complete self-sacrifice and devotion". "Many among them lead the life of hermits, of a type most in harmony with the Indian mentality. They devote themselves to the social and economic advancement of their converts no less than to their religious care, identifying themselves completely with them and their country. This gives them the greatest influence over the lives and character of their flock."[6] This refers to Catholic as much as to Protestant missionaries. Simon Bara wrote that the simple, genuine, undemonstrative love shown

---

[6] Quoted from W. Koppers, loc. cit., p. 281.

to them by the missionaries attracted his people more than many other things they did for them, or their heroic sacrifices or their erudition. This applies to the Western missionaries. What often impresses most is that the Western missionary has left his own country to live in remote regions in poverty, working without reward and often in danger of his life and yet neither despairing nor failing. More than once have natives surrounded the houses of Catholic missionaries at night in order to find out whether they really led celibate lives – could that be possible? – only to find out with astonishment that the missionaries were, in fact, celibate. I have been told that in India Christians trust European more than Indian priests; and in China I learned that Christians prefer European to Chinese bishops.

CHAPTER NINE

CONCLUSIONS

Learning from Criticism

WE trust that our analysis has shown that Christianity in Asia is a factor to be reckoned with. It cannot be overlooked; it calls for a decision. It stirs our imagination and our thinking despite the many distorted, false and unfavourable criticisms of the Christian religion. Indifference would indeed be worse than false judgements. Men who persecute and fight Christianity are more easily brought to the faith than those who think nothing about it. St. Paul, who persecuted Christ, came to him in the end, unlike Pilate who was indifferent to truth, or at least thought it unattainable. It was the German writer Paul Landsberg who said that even our delusions may constitute a tragic path to truth from which those who are indifferent remain barred. Those Asians who praise the West and Western Christianity without reservation and try to ape Western models render Christianity no service. No one surrenders his own deepest values easily and without falling quickly into error.

There has been a great advance in Asian knowledge of the Christian faith. Much more than its externals are being noticed and examined by Asians. It would be an exaggeration to say that all the criticisms Asians make are typically Asian. In their view of Western Christianity and of the Christian religion in general they are largely in agreement with the non-Christians of other continents, and have derived many of their opinions from Europe or the United States. Among the motives that lead them to look so critically at Christianity is a genuine desire for truth and real devotion, for salvation, redemption and peace. Also the defence of their own national character and religion plays a large part. Some criticize in a spirit of good will and charity, others from ill will; some see faults and failures because they want them put right, others merely show them up.

In their examination of Christianity Asians have not so far arrived at any favourable result. The favourable opinions we have heard often came from the relatively best informed people and were invariably the most unbiased, yet on the whole adverse criticism predominates. For a long time we have looked down upon Asians. Now they have turned the tables on the West. They do not deny there are certain truths and values in the Christian faith, but its defects are held to be greater and more numerous. Western Christianity mainly is on trial but so is the Christian religion as such. Much of what is supposed to be specifically Western is essentially Christian, for instance, the belief in its absolute claims. To attack Western Christians on this score is to attack the Christian faith as such.

What Asians think and say about the Christian faith is to a large extent due to its own representatives. Many harsh and unfavourable opinions have their roots in bitter experiences. There are the crusades, colonialism, Western wars in Asia, bad examples set by Europeans and the effects of the philosophy they have instilled. The West has shattered the old order of Asia and has sown unrest.

Other criticisms are connected with the religious truth and values of the Christian faith itself. Both favourable and unfavourable opinions arise from these. Our Lord himself in his own lifetime never met with full understanding among the people, in some points not even among his own apostles. To the natural man Christianity remains so much foolishness and scandal. It is part of the essence of the true Church to be in a minority and to be despised and oppressed by the world. Where Christianity is not judged in the light of grace, misunderstandings are inevitable. If Christianity were nowhere "a sign which shall be contradicted" (Luke 2:34) and an object of misunderstanding, it would indeed be a symptom that we do not possess the only lasting truth, the one and only Mediator, the true Church; that we do not belong to Christ who was not even understood by those nearest to him. "Woe to you when man shall bless you" (Luke 6:26). It is our glory to have adhered to truth in the face of opposition, and to have preserved the universal Church in face of purely tribal and national religions.

Many opinions can be accounted for by the subjective experience, character, mental attitudes, heritage, environment, past and destiny of individual Asians and of the Asian nations alike. If one keeps in mind, for example, the extremely powerful influence and the effects of polytheism, theopanism and other non-Christian creeds in Asia, it is easy to realize the difficulties Asians will have in arriving at a proper and full understanding of Christianity.

Human wickedness also accounts for much. Sinners will always regard the Christian faith as an accusation and retaliate with counter charges. Many superficial minds will always tend to criticize and denigrate Christianity because they wish to justify themselves.

The basic question whether these Asian views of Western Christianity are justified is, however, of vital importance for the West. Much of what Asians say and think in their

CONCLUSIONS

ignorance may be wrong. Many among them have only an insufficient knowledge of the Christian faith and are seldom able to grasp anything that is alien to them, for instance, the Bible, Christian doctrine, the structure of the Church, or the sacramental life. In this context we may apply Pascal's saying: "Worldly things must first be known in order to be loved; divine things, in order to be known, must first be loved."

However, Asians are able to have a proper perspective because they are detached and thus able to see distinctly and clearly. But the defects of Western Christianity are only too frequently unjustly identified with the Christian faith as such. Only very few can distinguish between the Christian faith and its Western forms. As a rule the fact is also overlooked that many Western evils do not spring from Christianity but precisely from its rejection. It is true that Asians can retort that there is much talk still of Christian Europe and the Christian West. It would make things much easier if the fiction of "Christian nations" or "Catholic countries" could be dropped.

The Influence of Criticism

The power of ideas is unlimited. Asian ideas of Western Christianity undoubtedly have their effect on Asians as well as Westerners, Christians and non-Christians alike.

Only a tiny fraction of the population of the largest continent is Christian, and still smaller is the number of Catholics. Among the 1500 million inhabitants of Asia only forty-five to fifty million are Christians and of these only thirty-two million are Catholics. Neither in the ancient world nor during the middle ages or in our own era has the West attained successes in Asia even remotely resembling the Christianization of Europe. Most of the territories which had once been conquered – Palestine, Syria, Asia Minor, Armenia, Persia – have been lost. Christians in Asia to-day are proportionately less numerous than, for instance, in the fifth and sixth centuries, and their numbers show a smaller percentage of increase than that of the non-Christian population of Asia. Indeed, Asian populations which are particularly religious offer the most vigorous opposition. Indians are imbued with a very profound religious feeling; they have the finest understanding of the reality of the transcendental world, but they resist the Christian life most stubbornly.

There are several reasons for this "failure". The masses are subject to the force of inertia. From habit they remain where they are. Yet many deliberately reject Christianity. Their reasons are often based on unfavourable ideas of Christianity in particular. The close connection between Christianity and the West is a great disadvantage. It was useful while the "European fever" lasted. Now that the fever has passed, it is positively harmful. Their opposition to Christianity is by no means decreasing. The era in which Asians used to depreciate their own religions has been followed by an age of growing self-confidence. Europeans played a not insignificant part in this turn of events. European scholars and friends of Asia trained Asians in the study and appreciation of their countries' past, their ancient literature and art. Many Europeans have even been converted to Buddhism, Hinduism and Islam. This has increased the self-confidence of Asians and has greatly strengthened their belief in their own religions.

Shintoism, too, has expanded. Before the last war, Japanese thought was more than ever concerned with Amaterasu, the Sun goddess and ancestress of the imperial family and the nation, and with Tenno, who rules the Japanese isles by divine command of Amaterasu. More Japanese were visiting the holy shrines devoted to ancestor-worship. Shintoism found footholds in Korea, in Manchuria and in the islands occupied by the Japanese. Amaterasu was hailed in the old Manchurian national anthem. But great changes have taken place. The Emperor is no longer a "kami", yet Shinto still has life and is even re-generating itself.

In Buddhism, Hinduism and Islam resistance to

Christianity also in stiffening. Men like Ramakrishna, Vivekananda, Gandhi, Tagore and Ibn Saud have strengthened belief in the old religions, which found political backing in the newly-established Asian states.

The continued adherence to the traditional non-Christian religions is coupled with the endeavour for liberation from all potential Christian influence. There was a time when numerous Asians had the impression that Christianity was superior to their ancient religions, and adopted from it all kinds of ideas, values, desires and methods. In this respect as well the "European fever" has come to an end; and liberation from all that is foreign, return to Asian ideas and customs, re-examination of their own wisdom and world of values are the watchwords.

In 1906 Gandhi wrote words to the effect that to find salvation, India would have to forget all that it had learned during the last fifty years. Railways, telegraph lines, hospitals, lawyers, doctors, etc. must disappear altogether, and the so-called upper classes must learn to lead the life of the simple peasant, conscientiously, devoutly and thoughtfully, for they must recognize that only this kind of life provides true happiness. Most people do not go as far as that. In general Asians are more than ever anxious to imitate the technical achievements of Europe and America. Westernization, however, is considered as a purely temporary measure. The idea is to defeat the West with its own technique in order to live afterwards in truly Eastern fashion. In religious matters, however, many of them wish to remain or to be free from Europe.

Asians are not only prepared to value, defend and improve their own religions; they want to export them to Europe and America. Here there is a marked sense of mission. Mr. Vasvami, professor at Bombay University, declared in 1910: "Present-day India has a message for both the world and for Europe. The services that the West has rendered to India are known; but very few people know that India, too, has much to offer to the West. It opens up the sources of that inspiration of which the world is so sorely in need." India's message, he continued, is threefold: "It proclaims . . . the immediate union with the self-revealing spirit, synthesis of all world religions, and . . . the brotherhood of man that is identical with the Son of God." That remains true to-day. In the meantime, the sense of mission in certain groups of the Indian people has by no means decreased.[1]

This development has already had its effect. During the last centuries, Christianity in Asia was on the offensive. Unusually large forces were brought in, and the non-

[1] See *The Message and Mission of Indian Culture*. Extracts from the writings of Sri Aurobindo, compiled by Dr. Indra Sen (Pondicherry).

223

Christian religions were seriously endangered. Their capitulation appeared to be merely a matter of time; the structure of Hinduism, Buddhism, Confucianism had become derelict, not to mention the creeds of the primitive races; this, at least, was the impression gained by most European observers and reporters. Here important changes have taken place. Now Christianity is attacked along the whole line, and much time and energy has to be spent on its defence – both in Europe and in Asia. There are not only Christian missions in Asia, but Hindu, Buddhist and Islamic missions in Europe and America as well.

Yet however strong the movements against Christianity may be, there are certain Christian ideas and values – for instance monotheism and monogamy – which even those Asians who fight for the preservation of the Asian way of life and for the elimination of Christian influences cannot and will not combat.

It is only natural that Asian Christians cannot remain completely uninfluenced by the views on Western Christianity prevailing in their continent. Lapses from Christianity into paganism are not infrequent in Asia. For these, public opinion which is unfavourable to Christianity is certainly not always responsible; but in many cases it is the cause or at least partly so. The famous Indian writer Brahmabandhav Upadhyaya stopped before taking the ultimate step, but died as a Christian. Others, however, motivated by their disappointments, continued on their way. We mention only the well-known writer Faris As-Sidiaq (d. 1887), who, originally a Maronite, became a Protestant missionary and ended up as a Moslem; and Lin Yutang, whose books have been translated into many languages. Other Christians, inspired by a sense of superiority and pride as long as Christianity was generally regarded as ideal, have wavered under the pressure of public opinion. While Christianity was generally considered the ideal, they felt secure, superior and proud. Now recognizing the failings of Christians and the dangerous position of Christianity, they have lost this feeling to a great extent.

There are, however, sufficient numbers of Christians whose belief in Christianity as well as their loyalty remain unshaken by adverse opinions; their efforts aim largely at a more or less thorough separation from the European pattern of Christianity and a stronger emphasis on their own nature and traditions.

We European Christians, too, have not been completely uninfluenced by public opinion in Asia. Many believe that Asia has a message for us. As in ancient times, many Europeans expect salvation from the East. Men like Vivekananda, Tagore and Sadhu Sundar Singh have attracted large numbers of followers and have been much applauded. Books on Asian "saints" like Ramakrishna have become best-sellers. Buddhist groups exist in many Western cities. Some Europeans have become converts to Buddhism. During and after the Crusades and in the age of humanism, the East exercised a powerful influence on the West. The same is happening in our day when, for instance, Yoga is widely recommended in the West.

Those who can least afford to disregard Asian views on Christianity are the missionaries. They must listen all the time and seek the answers for themselves and for those entrusted to their care. The character of a missionary may indeed be formed by such exchanges. The ideas and feelings of the modern missionary are very different from those of his predecessors in the past century and also from those of Christians in Europe. Thus, for example, nearly all missionaries at one time were convinced of the superiority of Western culture over the civilizations of Asia. To-day many have become uncertain.

The effects of Asian public opinion on Christianity as such have hardly become manifest, although we may consider these views and have to make up our minds about them. The advantage is that the Western conscience will become more sensitive and the nature of the Christian faith itself clearer. We may indeed live to see a transformation of Christianity in Asia and in the world in general. When the Germanic tribes received and accepted the gospel they took it up in their own way and formed their own Christian pattern. The nations of Asia may do the same. Just as the Reformation served as an occasion for genuine reforms in the Church, Asia may in a similar way serve the Church.

Hitherto Asian thought has not resulted in any expansion or deepening of Western theology. In times to come, however, it may well bring about the recovery of parts of Catholic teaching which have been lost in the past, and may lead to new definitions of Christian doctrine. Theology may develop in the future with the aid of systems such as those employed by Ramanuja or other Oriental thinkers, as it developed in the past under the influence of Aristotelianism. A beginning was made a few decades ago by men like Upadhyaya Brahmabandhav, and to-day scholars like Father Johanns, S. J. work on the same lines.

So far Asian views and opinions have provided little or no reason for changes or reforms in our devotions and worship. The various denominations in Europe and America as well as in Asia in general adhere to their traditions. There is as yet no trace of any influence of, say, the Indian methods of meditation or the Japanese symbolism of colours. Much the same can be said of the moral life of Christians. Its criticism by Asians is, to a large extent, justified and contains an element of truth. All the same conditions have not changed.

Practical Applications

Much can certainly be learned from Asian views of Western Christianity. They may help Western Christians to understand themselves, their doctrine and conduct, their pastoral and mission work. Western Christians must stop imagining that they cannot learn from the East. They must once and for all discard a pride that is contrary to the Christian faith. Mr. J. C. H. Wu wrote in *Beyond East and West*: "The West has something to learn from the East, for on the whole the East has gone further in natural contemplation than the West in its supernatural contemplation."

Asian criticisms have revealed to us our special characteristics. They make us see the difference between Western Christianity and Christianity as such. Forcefully we are reminded that Western Christianity in many respects is only one form of the Christian faith and that the latter may adopt other patterns; at the same time they will be reminded that by virtue of their past history they have something to give to Asia.

CONCLUSIONS

What Asians think about Western Christianity will be of increasing importance to theology, especially the new science of missiology. In the past historical accounts of missionary activities invariably suffered from onesidedness. Reports from missionaries, the Vatican archives and second-hand information constituted the main sources. What the people to be converted felt or said was only rarely considered. Besides scarcely anything was recorded apart from the missionaries' own activities, their own motives and interests. The reactions to these, what caused these reactions and what was their purpose were not investigated. There is not a single history of the missions with a satisfactory interpretation of Asian reactions. As far as Christian apologetics are concerned, they cannot do to-day without a study of comparative religion. The traditional superficial knowledge of other religions no longer suffices. Dogmatic theology, too, ought to study and discuss the Asian point of view.

We may also learn to improve our own attitude. This need not mean that we ought to swallow the current cliché about the declining West and the ascending East, or indeed that we might wish to see Christianity replaced by Eastern religions. Neither the enlightenment of Buddha, nor the wisdom of Laotse, nor the sober morality of Confucius can satisfy and help us. What we have had to say should not lead to the conclusion that we ought to go back to the very beginnings of the Christian faith. The synthesis of Christianity and Greek civilization, for instance, cannot be regarded as a deflection from the right path, nor the link of Christianity with Western civilization as a development in the wrong direction. It is not our conclusion that the essence of Christianity should be changed and alien ideas grafted on to it.

Yet we shall note what Asians have to say about Western moral and religious shortcomings. There can be no doubt that the European and American ways of life have had a frustrating effect on the Asian missions. "The name of God through you is blasphemed among the Gentiles" (Rom. 2:24). I was told by a bishop in the Far East that he would much rather have no white men at all in his diocese; it would make his work much easier. The white people with their irreligious life cause too much scandal. More preaching without words is needed. An exemplary Christian life is the missionary's best method. Rabindranath Tagore said to a missionary: "Do not try to preach new doctrines, but give yourself in charity. . . . Every Christian should be like Christ. . . . You cannot preach Christ until you yourself have become like Christ." A schoolmaster said at a conference of Indian teachers: "Many among you are Christians. If all of you lived like Christ the whole of Asia would be at your feet to-morrow."

Western priests may well be deeply depressed in view of these criticisms of their faith by Asian non-Christians. They need not despair of Western Christianity and their own ministry. Men and nations can be cured, but we must take to heart many of the accusations made by Asians, and act accordingly.

Many who know Asia, or profess to know it believe all missionary activity to be wrong. The entire mould of thought, as well as the mental attitude of Asians, they argue, cannot be changed and is incompatible with Christianity. We should, therefore, give up all missionary work. I do not agree, though I think missions and pastoral work in Asia should differ from those in Europe and Africa. There is no denying the fact that Western Christianity strikes many Asians as strange. It has been suggested that Christianity should be translated back into the oriental shape of its beginnings, and that the missions in Asia should be handed over to Christians who are closer to the Asians than we are. It is difficult to find the right answer. We do not know God's ways. We may mention in passing that many believe and expect that Russia, which has moved towards Asia, may in future create a pattern of Christianity better adapted to the Asian mind. My personal belief is that European Christianity still has a mission to fulfil in the East. Someone who knew India well wrote: "If you sever the Christians of India from all Western influences, they will become a Hindu caste, worshipping Christ as an incarnation of Vishnu whose priest is the Brahmin." Much the same could be said of the position of Christianity in other Asian countries.

Those who desire or demand the withdrawal of Western missionaries ought to remember that until quite recently leading Asians have declared that foreign missionaries were needed. Before the war Bishop Hayasaki told me in Nagasaki that foreign priests were still in demand to demonstrate the unity and universality of the Church to the Japanese. Cardinal Tien and Archbishop Yupin of Nanking said the same of the Church in China. But only those missionaries are wanted who set aside all Western feelings of superiority and are prepared for humble service.

We should carefully and objectively examine Asian criticism and accept it for the sake of souls. All true knowledge, all genuine religious forces and non-religious values ought to be recognized for what they are worth. The nations of Asia have to make their contribution towards the interpretation of Christ's message and to express it in the manner best suited to them. Dr. Hsiao has rightly said that the West was as one-sided as Asia. A synthesis was needed, but only Christians could bring it about.

One last point. Our investigations have shown that the struggle between the Asian religions and Christianity has by no means yet penetrated to the heart of the matter or reached its climax. The main conflict and the final decisions are still to come. We must expect the spiritual conflict to increase and deepen and paganism to become much more conscious of itself. There will be a powerful anti-Christian trend and it will be against Christ, motivated by more than mere habit. The task of the missions will become still more difficult.

More than forty years ago Rudolf Otto pointed out that the religions of the East would, under the impact of the Christians missions, begin to reflect, to renew themselves and to rally; but this was only the beginning. "A gigantic struggle is about to take place. We look forward to a time when mankind will have overcome its convulsions. Perhaps it will come sooner. I envy the men destined to see that day. It will be the most solemn and sublime moment in the history of mankind when political systems, economic groups and social interests will rise against each other no longer, but when the great religions of mankind will enter the arena. After the early conflicts about the shells and crusts of myth and dogma, about accidents of history, the climax will be reached when ultimately spirit will be pitted against spirit, ideal against ideal, experience against experience; when each man must reveal without deception the depth of his heart, and whether he has a heart at all."

Meanwhile the struggle has become more intense and we are reaching its climax. The Christian missionary movement in Asia as we have known it is, according to one Chinese writer,[2] "a closed chapter". He considers its present suspension to be a prelude to a brighter and richer missionary movement, a new type of missionary effort which will start in the very heart of Communist China. As far as the future of the Asian continent with its fifteen hundred million inhabitants is concerned there can be no Christian withdrawal. We are not at the end but only at the beginning of the Asian mission.

[2] Chan, Religious Trends in Modern China (New York, 1953).

BIBLIOGRAPHY

AKHILANANDA	*Hindu View of Christ*. New York, 1949.
ALSDORF, L.	*Indien*. Berlin, 1940.
ANESAKI, M.	*Religious Life of the Japanese People*. Tokyo, 1938.
APPASAMY, A. J.	*Christ in the Indian Church*. Madras, 1935.
ASAD MUHAMMAD	*The Road to Mekka*. New York.
AUROBINDO, SRI	*The Divine Life*. 1951.
	The Message and Mission of Indian Culture. Extracts from the writings of Sri Aurobindo compiled by I. Sen. Pondicherry, s. a.
BERDIAIEV, N.	*The Meaning of History*. London, 1930.
BUCK, O. M.	*Our Asiatic Christ*. New York and London, 1927.
BÜRKLER, X.	*Die Sonn- und Festtagsfeier in der katholischen Chinamission*. Rome, 1942.
CHAN, W.	*Religious Trends in Modern China*. New York, 1953.
CHANTEPIC DE LA SAUSSAYE	*Lehrbuch der Religionsgeschichte*. Two vols. Tübingen, 1925.
ESTBORN, S.	*The Religion of Tagore in the Light of the Gospel*. Madras, 1949.
FISCHER, S.	*Wanderfahrten eines Kunstfreundes in China und Japan*. Stuttgart-Berlin, 1939.

GABRIEL, W. *Gandhi, Christus und wir Christen.* Halle a. d. Saale, 1931.

GANDHI *Der Heilige und Staatsmann in eigenen Aussprüchen.* Selected and introduced by B. P. L. Bedi and Father M. Houlston. Munich, 1933.

HEILER, FR. *Christlicher Glaube und indisches Geistesleben.* Munich, 1926.
Die buddhistische Versenkung. Munich, 1922.
Sadhu Sundar Singh. Munich, 1926.

HUH SHIH AND LIN YUTANG *China's Own Critics.* Peiping, 1931.

KARRER, O. *Das Religiöse in der Menschheit und das Christentum.* Freiburg i. Br., 1934.

KITAYAMA, J. *West-östliche Begegnung.* Berlin, 1941.

KRÄMER, A. *Christus und Christentum im Denken des modernen Hinduismus.* Bonn, 1958.

KRAEMER, H. *The Christian Message in a Non-Christian World.* London, 1938.

KU HUNG MING *Chinas Verteidigung gegen europäische Ideen.* Jena, 1911.

LACOMBE, O. *Chemins de l'Inde et philosophie chrétienne.* Paris, 1956.

LINDEMANN, H. *Der Islam im Aufbruch, in Abwehr und Angriff.* Leipzig, 1941.

MUSHARRAF MOULAMIA KHAN *Pages in the Life of a Sufi.* London, 1932.

NISHIDA, KITARO	*Die intelligible Welt.* Berlin, 1943.
OGATA K. UND S. HEYER	*Vom Glauben des japanischen Volkes.* Marburg, 1943.
PANIKKAR, K. M.	*Asia and the Western Dominance.* London, 1953.
PAUL, L.	*Zweierlei Flamme.* Basle, 1939.
RADAKRISHNAN, S.	*Die Lebensanschauung der Hindu.* Leipzig, 1928.
	East and West in Religion. London, 1949.
	Indian Philosophy. Two vols. London, 1948.
ROSENKRANZ, G.	*Buddha und Christus im Ringen um die Seele Chinas.* Gütersloh, 1941.
	Fernost — Wohin? Heilbronn, 1941.
SARMA, S.	*Studies in the Renaissance of Hinduism.* Benares, 1944.
	Our Heritage and its Significance. Bombay, 1947.
SAUNDERS, K.	*The Gospel of Asia.* London, 1928.
SCHMIDLIN, J.	*Das gegenwärtige Heidenapostolat im fernen Osten.* Two parts in one volume. Münster i. Westf., 1929.
SCHOMERUS, H. W.	*Buddha und Christus.* Halle a. d. Saale, 1931.
	Indien und das Christentum. Three parts. Halle a. d. Saale, 1931–3.
	Indische und christliche Enderwartung und Erlösungshoffnung. Gütersloh, 1941.
SCHŬEJ-OHASAMA AND A. FAUST	*Zen.* Gotha-Stuttgart, 1925.

SCHÜTTE, J.   *Die katholische Chinamission im Spiegel der rotchinesischen Presse*. Münster i. Westf., 1957.

STRÖLE, A.   *Gandhi und die Religion*. Stuttgart, 1933.

SUNDAR SINGH   *Das Suchen nach Gott*. Munich, 1925.

SUZUKI, D. T.   *Die große Befreiung*. Leipzig, 1939.

TAGORE, R.   *Nationalismus*. Munich, 1921.
Sadhana. German translation by H. Meyer-Frank. Munich, 1921.

TAI HSU   *Lectures in Buddhism*. Paris, 1928.

TAO PUNG FAI   *Chinas Geist und Kraft*. Breslau, 1935.

VAN STRAELEN, H.   *The Far East must be Understood*. London, 1945.
Through Eastern Eyes. Loveland, Ohio, 1957.

WALTER, G.   *Gottes Kampf auf gelber Erde*. Paderborn, 1938.

WEI   *The Spirit of Chinese Culture*. New York, 1947.

WINSLOW, J. C.   *Christian Yoga or the Threefold Path of Union with God*. London, 1923.
The Indian Mystic. London, 1926.

WINTERNITZ, M.   *Rabindranath Tagore*. Prague, 1936.

WU, J. C. H.   *Beyond East and West*. New York and London, 1952.

ZIMMER, H.   *Anbetung mir*. Munich and Berlin, 1929.

GLOSSARY

Accommodation: Technical term in missiology, meaning the adaptation of Christian doctrine, worship etc. to the different peoples

Ahimsa: Harmlessness or non-violence, respect for all life

Amaterasu: Sun-goddess of Shintoism

Amida: Japanese name for Amitabha (= infinite light), one of the five eternal Buddhas in Mahayana-Buddhism

Arya Samaj: "Society of Aryas", founded in India by Dayanand Sarasvati (d. 1883)

Ashram: 1. stages of life in Hinduism. 2. an Indian community, whose members live together

Atman: In Indian philosophy and religion the individual soul (breath) or the one universal, all-comprising soul

Avataras: Incarnations of gods (Vishnu) in Hinduism

Bhagavadgita: "Song of the Lord". Indian poem, included in the epic Mahabharata

Bhakti: Devotion to a personal god, love, a mean of salvation in Hinduism

Brahma (masculine): Hindu, god member of the Hindu triad (trimurti)

Brahman (neuter): In Hinduism the Absolute, the universal supreme Spirit

Brahmanism: Religion of India in the post-vedic time, from which has developed the modern Hinduism

Brahmo-Samaj: Reformed, monotheistic branch of Hinduism, founded by Ram Mohan Roy (d. 1883)

239

Devadasis: Temple women, religious prostitutes, "brides of the gods" in India

Europeanism: The import of the western form of Christianity in the missions

Fakir: A religious beggar (Islam)

Gita: see Bhagavadgita

Hinayana: "Lesser Vehicle", the Theravada or Pali Buddhism of Ceylon, Burma, Thailand, Cambodia, Laos, the older and more conservative type of Buddhism

Hotoke: Japanese word for the Buddhas and Bodhisattous

Ismailia: Islamic sect (Shia), founded in the ninth century, believing in the coming of Messiah or Mahdi

Jana: Final stage in the mysticism of the Sufis (Islam)

Jodo-Shinshu: School of Japanese Buddhism

Ju: Chinese word for Confucius

Kami: Shinto gods

Krishna: God of Hinduism

Kwanon: Japanese name for Kuan yin (Chinese), the goddess of mercy

Lama: "Superior", name for lamaist monks of higher ranks

Lamaism: The Mahayana Buddhism of Central Asia (Tibet etc.)

Mahayana: "Great Vehicle", the Buddhism of Central Asia, China, Korea, Japan, Vietnam

Moslem: A follower of Mohammed (adherent to Islam)

Mudras: Gestures of prayer

Nichiren-shu: A sect of Japanese Buddhism, founded by Nichiren (d. 1282)

Nirvana: The state of the enlightened in Buddhism

Parsees: The modern Zoroastrians

Puranas: Books of Hinduism

GLOSSARY

Sadharan Brahmo Samaj: Branch of the Brahmo Samaj

Sadhu: "Pious", "pure", "saint": the ascetic and sage of Hinduism

Samsara: Round of rebirth in Hinduism

Secularism: Disbelief in the existence of God or gods, belief only in this world, "Weltfrömmigkeit"

Shaktas: Indians who worship the shakti (power) of a goddess, seeing in her the highest principle

Shivaism: Branch of Hinduism

Sufism: The mysticism of Islam

Syncretism: Union of contradicting religious doctrines etc.

Synthesis: Reconciliation of different religious doctrines etc. in a higher unity

Tao: "Way", technical term in Taoism, Confucianism. Can not be defined exactly

Taoism: A Chinese religion, claiming to be founded by Laotse

Tao te king (Tao te ching): The classic book of Taoism, attributed to Laotse

Tenno: Title of the Japanese Emperor

Theopanism: Doctrine, that God is all. Extreme contrast to Pantheism (the All is God)

Tien: "Heaven", name for the highest god in Confucianism centre of the Confucian state religion

Vedanta: "End of the Veda", one of the orthodox systems of Hindu philosophy

Vishnuism: Branch of Hinduism

Yoga: 1. One of the orthodox systems of Hindu philosophy. 2. way of mental concentration

Zen: 1. "Meditation", cultivated in the Zen-school of Buddhism. 2. Japanese school of Mahayana-Buddhism

INDEX

INDEX